FEMINISING THE MARKET

Feminising the Market

Women's Pay and Employment in the European Community

Jane Pillinger

First edition 1992
Reprinted 1993

Published by
THE MACMILLAN PRESS LTD
Houndmills, Basingstoke, Hampshire RG21 2XS
and London
Companies and representatives
throughout the world

ISBN 0–333–56335–2 hardcover
ISBN 0–333–59835–0 paperback

A catalogue record for this book is available
from the British Library.

Printed in Hong Kong

For my mother, Angela

Contents

Contents

List of Figures

List of Tables

Abbreviations

ACAS	Advisory, Conciliation and Arbitration Service
APEX	Association of Professional, Executive, Clerical and Computer Staff
CA	Court of Appeal
BIFU	Banking, Insurance and Finance Union
CAC	Central Arbitration Committee
COREPER	Committee of Permanent Representatives
CPSA	Civil and Public Services Association
CREW	Centre for Research on European Women
DG	Directorate General
EAT	Employment Appeals Tribunal
EC	European Community
ECJ	European Court of Justice
ECR	European Court Reports
EETPU	Electrical, Electronic, Telecommunication and Plumbing Union
EIRR	*European Industrial Relations Review*
ENOW	European Network of Women
EOC	Equal Opportunities Commission
ERDF	European Regional Development Fund
ESF	European Social Fund
ETUC	European Trades Union Congress
ICR	Industrial Court Reports
IDS	Income Data Service
ILRIB	*Industrial Relations Legal Information Bulletin*
IRLR	*Industrial Relations Law Review*
IRRR	*Industrial Relations Review and Report*
JES	Job Evaluation Study
LRD	Labour Research Department
NALGO	National Association of Local Government Officers
NUTGW	National Union of Tailors and Garment Workers
OJ	*Official Journal of the European Communities*
PAB	*Pay and Benefits Bulletin*
PSI	*Public Services International*
TASS	Technical, Administrative and Supervisory Section of the Engineers' Workers Union

TUC   Trades Union Congress
UCATT   Union of Construction, Allied Trades and Technicians

Acknowledgements

There are many people who have made it possible for this book to become a reality. I have been given an enormous amount of support and help by people involved directly or indirectly with the European Community, in trade unions and the women's movement. In particular I would like to thank the many people who have let me interview them over the years in Brussels and Strasbourg, and for their time in giving me information.

My thanks also go to Sue Lonsdale and Jo Campling for their help and advice in getting this book into publication. I am also grateful to the European Commission for permission to reproduce the tables and charts contained in the book.

I would also like to thank my colleagues at Northern College who have supported me throughout the writing of this book and to my friends who have listened to my trials and errors and who have helped me to put the whole experience in perspective. My biggest thanks go to Jill Hirst, whose constant support, unique insights and belief in my ability to see an end to the book have been unfaltering.

JANE PILLINGER

1 Introduction

This book developed out of a long-standing interest in the potential and actual impact of the European Community (EC) on women.[1] EC policies to protect women at work, especially in the Single European Market, have responded to a concern that women start from an unequal position, compared to men, in their access to well-paid, secure employment. The advent of the Single European Market in 1992 has heightened these concerns and increasingly we are witnessing a 'European' rather than a 'national' approach to policy-making. However, the development of EC policy to protect and enhance women's roles in the labour market has not been prompted solely by the single market. Policies have developed over several decades as growing pressure from women and the greater visibility of women in the public realms of work and politics have insisted that women should no longer be left on the sidelines of work and society. The demands, pressure and lobbying of the European women's movement have played a vital, if often publicly unrecognised, role to achieve a better deal for women.

The feminisation of the EC labour market, especially in particular industries and occupations, has been matched at the EC level by the growing feminisation of policy-making. This has not necessarily led to significant gains for women as they enter or attempt to enter the more public worlds of work and as they become more visible in welfare policies. Thus the book's title reflects two different trends in Europe.

The first is that the world of paid work is increasingly becoming feminised. Although women in all EC countries make up a large part of the labour market, their roles in paid work, their skills and jobs performed are frequently marginalised and undervalued. Deregulation of labour markets across Europe has led to new forms of working patterns that particularly affect women. As a result 'Europe's work-force could become a huge, scarcely differentiated pool of casual labour . . . women are likely to be the main victims' (Huws, 1989). Accompanying the feminisation of the labour market we see the growing feminisation of poverty. Increased labour market participation has not always led to greater prosperity for women and the growing trend towards more atypical and flexible forms of employment frequently leaves women in vulnerable and insecure jobs. These

1

trends are enhanced by the single market where new forms of competition are spearheading the deregulation and casualisation of work. This is leading to worsening conditions of employment and social protection.

Second, the EC policy-making structure is becoming increasingly feminised. The contribution of the policies of the EC to protect and enhance women's job opportunities has been significant. Yet this progress has done little to secure better job opportunities, better relative pay and enhanced conditions of work for women.

1990 marked the beginning of a decade of change as Europe entered a new historic era brought about by German reunification, closer economic and political ties and the overthrow of communist regimes in Eastern Europe as well as the creation of the single market. Although the single market is confined to economic and monetary affairs the EC has sought increasing levels of social cohesion. At the same time this has brought with it a new politics of exclusion where vulnerable groups in the EC, for instance black and migrant workers, are being excluded from the benefits of closer European integration.

It is questionable how women, and particularly the most vulnerable groups of women in Europe, will reap the benefits that are being presented as a *fait accompli* for increased prosperity. The passing of the Single European Act in 1986 started a new debate about the role of social policy in the EC or, as it has become known, the 'social dimension'. The reservations shown within the Council of Ministers about a wide-ranging social dimension has been demonstrated by its reluctance to extend majority voting to social policies and particularly to policies affecting women's roles in European society. Nevertheless, it is anticipated that more and more decisions relating to economic and social legislation will rest with the EC. In 1988 Jacques Delors (President of the Commission) stated in the European Parliament that this could increase to 80 per cent of all social and economic policy.

This book sets out to examine the EC's policies affecting women and their implementation in practice. In particular it focuses on the impact of the Single European Market on women and how policies have been developed in the light of the changing role of Europe. An understanding of the historical development of EC policies affecting women's roles and status provides a context and understanding of developments in the 1990s.

Europe may have represented a loosely grouped set of countries tied together by geographic boundaries, as much based on common political, economic and defence interests as on different cultural, religious and social beliefs and organisation. However, it has increasingly come to be more than a means of securing common objectives in economic and military terms. The Single European Market has brought with it the knitting together of European economic and monetary policies, with objectives related to the improvement of living and working conditions for all (although this only includes those who are citizens in Europe). This has led to debates about the role of a 'social' Europe, of a European welfare state, and the need to ensure that all 'citizens' (though not necessarily all residents) are given the opportunity to share a minimum level of social protection. Coupled with this view of a common heritage and common political and economic objectives is the view that social policies invariably follow and bolster economic policy. The question of who is excluded and who is included in this approach will give an indication of the scope of European integration. Will this mean integration for all groups in the EC? How will it affect women, black and ethnic minority groups and migrant workers?

Patterns of women's pay, employment and social situations, while varying amongst the different EC countries, show some remarkable similarities. In all EC member states women work in low-paid, low-skilled jobs. Their work is consistently undervalued and they have poorer access to training than men. Their lives are constrained in EC countries by national social policies that restrict their integration into work, where strong assumptions are made about women as dependants, mothers and carers. In many senses women in Europe share similar experiences of patriarchy. Chapter 2 sets out women's pay and employment position in the EC and demonstrates the different factors that restrict their access to paid employment. It is evident from this that women start from a much weaker position in the labour market than men.

There is no doubt that women's pay and employment will be affected by the Single European Market. The redefinition of the organisation, value and status of work affects women and men differently. These changing patterns of work, brought about in part by the single market will have an impact on different groups of women. Skilled and mobile women will experience more opportunities, whilst working-class, black or migrant women could face even more restricted opportunities and exploitation. Chapter 3 provides an analysis of how the Single European Market affects women. It shows how the model of the white, skilled, mobile, male worker limits women's prospects for benefiting from the single market. A discussion on black women shows that the new fortress Europe will greatly disadvantage black women and migrant workers.

Women have increasingly taken a role in pressurising the EC to develop policies. Chapter 4 shows the different ways in which the EC has opened its doors to women and the various institutional and lobbying mechanisms women have developed to get themselves heard.

The EC has responded to some of women's specific needs by passing directives and other policy instruments. Chapter 5 provides the specific policies on women's pay and employment, their development and implementation, up to 1986. It shows why EC policy on equal pay has been too narrow a policy to improve the situation of women at work. This leads into an assessment of the more recent influences and pressures that have been placed on the EC to develop policies beyond equal pay, through a variety of directives and action programmes for women. It also shows how member governments have responded to these developments and the pressures placed on them. Chapter 6 shows how these developments have affected member states. By taking a case study of the implementation of the 1975 Equal Pay Directive, it is possible to gain some insight into the implementation of policy at a practical level in member states.

Chapter 7 looks at the policies that have been developed for women in the single market and critically assesses the EC in this light. It also questions how far the EC-level discussions about new models of work can benefit women. An assessment of the implementation of the Social Charter, passed in 1989, is provided in this context. The chapter highlights the need for a new European social policy that brings women's inequality to the centre of any debate about a new Europe. Chapter 8 goes on to show how trade unions and women's groups in Europe have responded to the single market and outlines their priorities for action to ensure that women do not lose out.

Finally, by looking at the role of the EC, its policies on women and the impact of the single market, the book develops a feminist analysis of the EC. It shows how the scope of EC policy has a limited and restricted definition of work that needs to be broadened to take account of the reality of women's lives, of their material, social and political roles. It will be shown that a framework needs to be developed to bring women to the centre of the debate about the single market and its social dimension. It will provide a new perspective for understanding women's rights in a European framework by demonstrating how the single market necessitates a new European focus for campaigns on women's rights.

Although we are told that the Single European Market is leading to new forms of economic prosperity, no indication is given of how women are expected to benefit from this. Will it lead to greater prosperity for women, or will it merely reinforce women's experience of inequality and disadvantage? Will women be given a say in how Europe is to be modelled and organised? Will it take account of the different experiences of all women, of black and migrant women, of lesbians, of disabled women, of single parents, and of older and younger women? Will national governments respond to the EC's policies for women in a positive way, or will they attempt to restrict these opportunities at the regional or national level? These questions will be addressed in the book. It is not expected that all of them will be answered. However, it is hoped that this book will provide an understanding of the developments taking place in Europe and how they are affecting women. It will show how the organisation of patriarchy has constructed the EC, just as it has constructed patriarchy at the national, regional and local level.

MODELS OF EUROPEAN WELFARE AND THE ROLE OF WOMEN

Although a common approach of postwar welfare states, the tradition of the interventionist role of the modern state in social policy is no longer taken for granted, nor viewed with a unified approach throughout the changing geography of Europe. Whilst increasing attention is being given to the growing use of models of European welfare, they are diverse in their make-up, especially when comparing postwar welfare developments in southern and northern European states, and as Eastern European countries grapple with new models. The point here is that there is no certainty that Europe will develop common patterns of social policy, nor that these will develop at a 'European' rather than at a national or regional level. The pattern of social policy development over the next few decades will increasingly be of concern to the European Community in its attempts to define the boundaries of a 'social' Europe, in contrast to the well-developed and well-defined notion of an 'economic' Europe. Crucial to this development will be the focus and priority given to groups in the population who do not immediately derive 'economic' benefits from the marrying of economic and monetary policies. What model of welfare will the EC develop and how responsive will it be to women's specific needs?

Analyses of welfare developments and models of welfare have frequently failed to give women visibility. The growing and developing body of feminist analyses of social policy has highlighted the frequent marginalisation of women in policy, the gender-neutral approaches of policy makers and the subordination with which many women are viewed in policy making (Dale and Foster, 1986; Pascall, 1986; Ungerson, 1985). The new development of comparative frameworks of feminist research has also highlighted the similarities and differences of social policies and their impact on women. Women's dependency, their roles in the family and their roles at work are patterned in similar ways across Europe. In this sense it is important to look at women's visibility in attempts to define the social boundaries of Europe, and in the development of models of European welfare states. Will these be unified or will they reflect the different characteristics of national policy making? Who will be the focus of these policies and will they bring women's concerns to the centre of policy making?

Analyses of welfare models for comparative purposes by Gøsta Esping-Andersen (1990) and Stephan Leibfried (1990) have identified several groupings of states or, to put it another way, 'regimes' of welfare, in Europe. Esping-Andersen characterises these as liberal, conservative and social democratic. Stephan Leibfried distinguishes between four different types of social policy regimes: the Scandinavian model, the Bismark model, the Anglo-Saxon model and the Latin Rim model.

Esping-Andersen's work builds on and extends the work of Titmuss's models of welfare by relating them to the changing conditions in western 'post-industrial' societies. Esping-Andersen's work assesses the extent to which the welfare state has an impact on class, with some implications for gender in his analysis. In particular he raises the question of the extent to which welfare regimes enable decommodification (or autonomy/independence from market forces).

Liberal regimes can be found in countries like the UK, where public provision is accompanied by state subsidising of private welfare programmes. It is characterised by a degree of universalism and social insurance, with selectivity and means testing for income maintenance of the non-working population. There is a strong work ethic behind income-maintenance policies. Countries like Germany, Austria, France and Italy are seen to fit into conservative regimes where the traditional corporatist model influenced by the Church and the corresponding emphasis on the role of the family shape social policies. The state becomes involved in the provision of social policy where the family is unable to provide for itself. In contrast social democratic regimes are more universal in emphasis, where individual rights are emphasised, rather than rights based on dependency within the family. The state takes an instrumental role in securing women's access to the labour market by providing childcare and by creating job opportunities within welfare services.

Although Esping-Andersen makes reference to gender, in particular when referring to the role of the family, women remain marginalised in his analysis. Mary Langan and Ilona Ostner's (1990) analysis of his work shows the accidental way in which women are included, and that his failure to theoretically address gender means that women are left on the sidelines in his comparative framework. As a result, they argue that the position of women in the labour market cannot be discussed without also examining women's roles in the family:

> Men are made ready for commodification (for bargaining in a market) by the women in the family. Women are decommodified by the position in the family. Thus women and men are 'gendered commodities' with quite different experiences of the labour market. (p. 6)

Stephan Leibfried takes on board some of these issues relating to women in distinguishing between four different types of social policy regimes: the Scandinavian model, the Bismark model, the Anglo-Saxon model and the Latin Rim model. These relate principally to social security 'regimes' and poverty policies which differ in their commitments to universalism or selectivity, their emphasis on employment policies and the right to work, their levels of modernisation, and religious traditions.

The Scandinavian 'modern' model has frequently been held as a model for universal notions of social citizenship, where labour market policies have been at the heart of the welfare state. The model is viewed as representing a modern welfare state and provides employment, especially for women. This is seen as an important source of income transfer. The Bismark 'institutional' model (Germany and Austria), in contrast, is defined as an institutional welfare state, where compensatory strategies for the non-working population are highlighted through basic rights to social security. Rather than the welfare state operating as an employer, it operates principally as a subsidiser. The Anglo-Saxon 'residual' model (increasingly including Britain and the USA) represents a system of residual welfare, where the indirect effects of residualism have the effect of forcing people into the labour market, rather than subsidising their entry through compensatory or labour market strategies. The Latin Rim 'rudimentary' model (including the southern European countries such as Spain, Portugal, Greece and to a lesser extent Italy) represents a rudimentary welfare state system, where rights to welfare are not necessarily guaranteed. Like the Anglo-Saxon model, this system is based largely on residualism and forced labour market entry, but has an historical tradition of welfare based on the Catholic Church. Although no tradition of full employment is evident in these countries, their constitutions do show evidence of moving towards a modern welfare state model.

Although gender is incorporated into Leibfried's models of welfare, for instance in showing the Bismark countries' emphasis on male models of full employment, and the high labour market participation of women in the Scandinavian welfare services, gender remains marginalised. This is particularly the case in his failure to include a gender perspective into the analysis of the Anglo-Saxon and Latin Rim countries, where women play a crucial role in providing 'hidden' welfare through the family and where women's labour market participation is correspondingly limited or fragmented. Mary Langan and Ilona Ostner (1990) argue that as a result the analysis 'fails to see one of the crucial factors in the way in which the four models can be organized as a continuum – from "rudimentary" to "modern"' (p. 11). As a result the basic organisation of welfare and the assumptions made about women's roles underpin our understanding of the very development of welfare.

Drawing on the work of Leibfried and Esping-Andersen, Langan and Ostner have attempted to develop a feminist framework, by integrating an analysis of the sexual division of labour, in the household, market or state. As a result rather than following the Scandinavian model, which liberates women and provides them with services to ensure that they compete equally with men for labour market participation, they move from personal dependency to state dependency. Women remain segregated in the labour market because their labour market integration has been largely in employment geared to providing the social services, for example childcare, to enable women to participate in the first place. Thus while social policies on the surface treat men and women equally and recognise that both men and women are potentially parents/carers through the individualised tax and wage policies and the policy of parental leave, these policies are only effective once women are in paid work. Once in paid work the services provided to enable women's labour market participation are provided by women.

The Bismarckian model is referred to as a gendered status-maintenance model, emphasising economic development and productivity alongside a central role for the family as the front line of care and services. The emphasis is on compensatory money transfers rather than on the provision of services. As in the Bismark model, women in the Anglo-Saxon model are viewed primarily as mothers, despite the fact that many of them are economically active. However, the state takes no role in providing services or directly encouraging women's labour market participation. Since the Anglo-Saxon model makes the assumption that everyone is the same (but not equal), and that no one group needs special services or programmes, it has the effect of creating inequalities. This is particularly enhanced by the emphasis on residualism in income-maintenance programmes – the view that it is a personal deficiency that leads to failure to compete equally in the labour market, not that structural barriers exist that prevent women from competing equally in the first place.

The Latin Rim countries are provisionally defined by Langan and Ostner as a 'mixed women's family support economy' where women play key 'invisible' roles in small firms and the underground economy. Rigid sexual divisions exist in work and family and women provide the bulk of welfare services within the family.

It is evident that despite differences between the various models discussed, they are underpinned by many similarities. Common to all of them is that women are viewed as resources for labour, reproduction and caring functions. Different welfare regimes place emphasis on these various functions in differing ways and the nature and effects of them are often crucial to women's labour market participation. However, it is clear that these are only effects and no one model demonstrates an understanding of the central focus that gender plays in welfare relations.

The foregoing discussion is important because it gives insight into the way in which the impact of the Single European Market on women can be examined. It necessitates an understanding of the 'invisible' and 'hidden' nature of women's roles in welfare, work and society. It also requires the development of a feminist analysis that brings women to the centre of discussions about the effects of the single market on women and the corresponding development and implementation of policy.

A number of questions are raised for the development of European policies on women. The first relates to the extent of diversity of welfare models in Europe. Are women viewed in similar ways and do social policies similarly reinforce women's inequality, subordination and dependence? Second, the possibilities for European rather than national social policies will have an impact on women in different ways in different countries. As different national welfare systems impact on women in different ways, how effective will EC policies on women be? Can the EC develop a coordinated set of policies that will impact on all women in all member states in similar ways? This leads to the third and related point. The conditions facing women's employment in the Single European Market will be determined by differing national social policies and their impact on women at the national level. For instance, those countries that provide good child-care, social infrastructure and training for women, through their national social policies, will be, at an individual and collective level, competitively stronger. At another level the provision of these social policies may affect the location of business and employment in the Single European Market and, therefore, employment and training opportunities for women.

This book addresses some of these issues and points to the ways in which the EC works to the advantage or disadvantage of women. It will show how EC policy on women is vital to ensure that distortions of competition and inadequate training and social infrastructure are redressed. For this reason a true Community can only be one that gives equal chances and opportunities to everyone. Otherwise, distortions of competition and merely paying lip service to women's contribution to the economy will exacerbate an already unequal Community.

Note

1. The European Community represents three separate communities. These are the European Coal and Steel Community (set up in 1952), the European Economic Community (set up in 1957) and Euratom (also set up in 1957). Although sharing the same institutions, they are bound by different Treaties. Policies relating to women's employment are derived from the European Economic Community, under the Treaty of Rome.

2 Women's Employment in the EC

The Single European Market is designed to facilitate free trade through the removal of physical, technical and human barriers. The effects the single market will have on women's employment have led women throughout Europe to feel concerned that new patterns of trade and monetary and economic policy will exacerbate women's vulnerable and unprotected patterns of work throughout the EC. Given that women start from a weaker position in the labour market than men, for instance in terms of pay and access to training and highly paid skilled work, they will equally be placed in a weaker position in competing for jobs, training and skilled work in the single market.

This chapter looks at the position of women in the labour market in the EC and shows that women start from a weaker position than men. A number of social and economic factors also affect women's access to employment. These include the continuing sex segregation of the labour market, the growing numbers of women involved in atypical forms of employment, women's lower pay relative to men's and their vulnerability to unemployment and underemployment. Domestic and childcare responsibilities and the inflexibility of the labour market to cater for women's specific needs interact with the vulnerable position of women in the labour market. In the context of this discussion the next chapter will look in more detail at what advantages or disadvantages the single market has for women.

WOMEN'S EMPLOYMENT IN THE EC

A large majority of women throughout the EC now expect to work, sometimes out of choice, but often out of necessity to prevent family poverty. Since the creation of the EC in 1957 women have entered the labour market in increasing numbers. In 1989, of a population of 167.3 million women, 51.4 million were in paid work in the EC. As a result women now represent a significant proportion of the EC labour market. In 1987 41.2 per cent of women worked in the EC, compared

11

to 36 per cent in 1980, with some countries having a higher proportion of women workers than others. Women's activity rates in the member states are shown in Figure 2.1. The highest activity rate is found in Denmark and the lowest in Spain. All EC labour markets saw a growth in women's activity between 1979 and 1988.

Table 2.1   Labour force participation rates of women in 1979, 1987 and 1995 (projected)

| | % | | |
	1979	*1987*	*1995*
Denmark	69.9	75.9	82.6
France	54.2	55.7	61.0
W. Germany	49.6	51.9	51.3
Greece	32.8	41.7	–
Ireland	35.2	38.5	39.8
Italy	38.7	43.4	47.7
Luxembourg	39.8	44.3	–
The Netherlands	33.4	41.9	52.3
Portugal*	57.3	57.4	58.5
Spain	32.3	37.5	–
UK	58.0	62.6	62.2
Belgium	47.4	52.0	–

* Includes persons under 15 years of age.
Source: Commission of the EC (1990b).

A larger proportion of all women now work and Table 2.1 shows women's labour force participation rates in 1979 and 1987 and the projected rates for 1995.

Moreover, women's share of employment grew at a faster rate than men's during the 1980s. Between 1987 and 1988 employment grew by just over 2 per cent for women, compared to just over 1 per cent for men. This is largely accounted for by a decline in male employment in traditional manufacturing industries and a corresponding increase in service sector activity, attracting largely female workers.

Women re-entering the labour market took up a substantial proportion of new jobs between 1986 and 1989, many of which were part-time. Higher growth rates throughout Europe contributed in part to higher levels of employment, which increased by 1.7 per cent in 1989. However, Gross Domestic Product has only risen by approx-

13

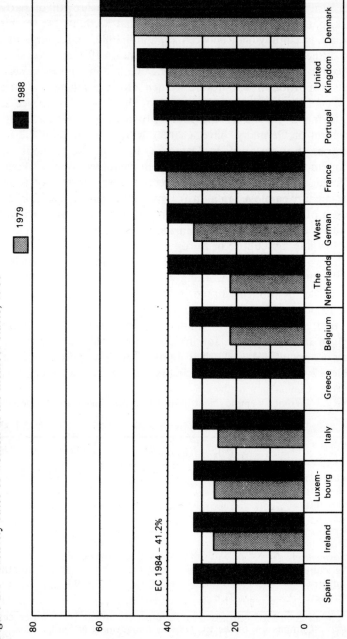

Figure 2.1   Activity rates of women in the member states, 1988

Source: Commission of the EC (1989a) *Employment in Europe*.

imately 3.5 per cent a year since 1986, a level which would not necessarily lead to new job creation. It is the growth of part-time work, particularly in the service sector, that accounts for the biggest increase in employment between 1986 and 1989, and a large proportion of the increase in women's employment. In 1989 approximately 60 per cent of people employed in the EC worked in the service sector, a large proportion of whom were women. However, there is a variation between EC countries in the extent of the growth in service sector employment. Inevitably the more prosperous countries, with the exception of Germany, have a larger service sector than the poorer countries. For instance, in Denmark and The Netherlands service sector employment is around 70 per cent compared to only 44 per cent in Portugal and 48 per cent in Greece. Larger numbers of people in Germany are employed in industry than in the service sector, largely as a result of a strong economy. This rise of the service sector in all EC countries coincided with a fall in the numbers of people employed in industry and agriculture in Europe.

The growth of the service sector throughout the EC has also led to a concentration of women working within the services. In 1988 just over 74 per cent of women worked in the service sector compared to just over 19 per cent in industry and 6.6 per cent in agriculture. Although the figures for agriculture underestimate the numbers of women engaged in that activity, for instance, due to farmers' wives' invisibility in agricultural work, their numbers are low and continue to fall. Table 2.2 shows women's participation in the three main employment

Table 2.2   Women's employment in agriculture, industry and the service sector, 1985–8

	1985	*1986*	*1987*	*1988*
Women employed in:				
(millions)				
Agriculture	3.7	3.5	3.5	3.3
Industry	9.4	9.4	9.5	9.7
Services	33.0	34.0	35.6	37.0
% share of				
employment in:				
Agriculture	8.0	7.5	7.3	6.6
Industry	20.5	20.1	19.8	19.3
Services	71.6	72.4	72.8	74.1

Source: Commission of the EC (1989a) *Employment in Europe.*

sectors from 1985 to 1988, and the corresponding decline of industrial and agricultural employment in favour of service sector employment. Within each branch of industry and the services women remain segregated from men, being concentrated in a narrow range of jobs. The growth of service sector employment, although increasingly feminised, has not opened up a vast range of new occupations for women. Women remain concentrated in welfare services and the caring professions, banking and insurance (largely as clerical workers), hotels and catering (in cooking and as domestic workers) and in retail distribution (as shop assistants). The larger the extent of welfare provision in each country the larger the participation of women in welfare-related jobs. For example, in Denmark over half of the women in paid work are employed in the public sector, many in the lower-skilled, lower-grade and lower-paid jobs. Likewise there are variations in the level of employment in banking and finance between EC countries. Banking and finance as well as business services account for more than 10 per cent of women's paid employment in Germany, France, Italy, the UK, Belgium, Luxembourg, The Netherlands and Spain. Seventy per cent of this employment is concentrated in Germany, the UK and France. In 1987 just over one million women were employed in the banking industry in the EC, with Germany, the UK and France accounting for 81 per cent of women's employment in banking.

Fewer women work in industry than in the services. However, their jobs are highly segregated from men's and are concentrated in a narrow range of occupations. Women are also likely to work in lower-skilled jobs than men and are frequently categorised as semi-skilled or unskilled. The sectors where women work are also highly feminised. For instance, 21 per cent of women's employment in industry in the EC is in clothing and textiles, an industry that has faced substantial restructuring and job losses since the 1970s. This is also a low-wage area of employment. In knitting and clothing, labour costs fall 20–40 per cent below the average labour costs in manufacturing for all EC countries.

WOMEN'S EARNINGS

Women in all EC countries continue to earn lower rates of pay than men in all employment sectors. Despite the introduction of equal pay legislation in all member states of the EC, women continue to earn on average up to one-third less than men. For example, women engaged in manual work in manufacturing earn on average one-quarter less than men. Broken down by member state in 1989, women earned 15 per cent less than men in Denmark and Italy, 20 per cent less in France and Greece, and 30 per cent less in the UK and Ireland.

Table 2.3 shows that there are significant differences between EC countries in pay between men and women. Although there has been a narrowing of the differential between men's and women's pay in all EC countries since 1973, this slowed down in the 1980s for all EC countries (excluding Belgium, Greece and France) and actually widened between 1979 and 1988 in Denmark and the UK. These figures only account for manufacturing and often exclude women working part-time or women employed by small firms. The lack of detailed statistics to assess the pay position of women in the service sector is a major gap in the actual pay position of all working women.

Table 2.3 Women's gross hourly earnings (in all industries) as a percentage of men's, 1975–88

	1975	*1977*	*1979*	*1981*	*1983*	*1985*	*1987/8*
Belgium	71.5	71.0	71.3	71.6	74.0	74.5	75.3
Denmark	–	–	86.4	85.8	85.5	86.3	75.3
France	78.5	77.4	78.3	79.4	80.1	80.8	80.8
Greece	69.9	68.4	68.0	66.7	74.6	78.8	78.7
Ireland	60.9	61.5	67.0	67.2	68.4	67.9	67.1
Italy	79.7	84.6	84.1	84.1	87.2	–	82.7
Luxembourg	63.2	65.0	61.9	63.4	65.0	66.1	66.9
The Netherlands	72.4	73.5	72.3	72.6	74.0	–	74.2
UK	67.9	71.6	70.8	70.0	69.5	–	68.9
W. Germany	72.6	72.8	72.7	72.6	72.8	73.0	73.4

Source: Eurostate Review, 1975–1984, 1976–1985; Eurostat: *Earnings in industry and services*, 1987/8 (Statistical Office of the European Communities).

A number of factors affect women's relative earnings. Although it is widely acknowledged that sex discrimination, often indirect, continues to be a major factor in determining differences in pay between men and women, this is an incomplete explanation. Women tend to work fewer hours than men, less overtime and are more likely to work part-time and and be employed by small firms. Women are also likely to be in lower-skilled jobs and have lower levels of seniority than men.

Moreover, pay is affected by both vertical and occupational segregation where women are employed in lower-grade jobs than men and in industries where levels of pay are low.

WOMEN AND UNEMPLOYMENT IN THE EC

It is very difficult to establish the actual rate of unemployment amongst women in the EC, since much of women's unemployment is hidden from official statistics. The large numbers of women who seek to re-enter the labour market after raising children is equally difficult to quantify. This also applies to the 'underemployment' of women. It is clear that women's labour is grossly underutilised:

Women are more likely than men to accept part-time or temporary casual work as an alternative to unemployment. Accepting a part-time or temporary job because a full-time or regular job is not available is an indicator of the involuntary character of these forms of working. (Commission of the EC, 1990b, p. 15)

Although women are becoming a growing proportion of the employed they are also becoming a growing proportion of the unemployed. This feminisation of unemployment is clear from the figures. In 1986 women represented 46 per cent of the unemployed in the EC, and this rose to 52 per cent in 1989. Like women's employment, their unemployment shows similar variations from country to country. For instance, women were 65 per cent of the unemployed in Portugal in 1989, compared to 37 per cent in Italy. Of particular importance is that women are representing a growing proportion of the long-term unemployed. In 1989 they represented about half of the long-term unemployed in the EC. This is a factor frequently hidden from the public gaze, and exacerbated by the restructuring of traditional areas of women's work, for example in clothing and textiles, in some regions of the EC.

The official rate of unemployment in the EC fell from nearly 11 per cent in 1986 to 9 per cent in 1989 (compared to rates of 5 per cent in the USA and 2 per cent in Japan in 1989). Women's rates of unemployment have remained higher than men's, but fell marginally from 13 per cent in 1986 to nearly 12 per cent in 1989, from 7.1 million to 6.7 million. Young women, aged 14–24, have continued to face higher rates of unemployment than young men. Table 2.4 shows the unemployment rates for men and women.

Table 2.4　Unemployment of men and women, 1986 and 1989

	1986	1989
Men and Women		
Unemployment rate	10.7	9.0
Youth unemployment rate (14–24)	22.3	17.4
Men		
Unemployment rate	9.2	7.0
Youth unemployment rate (14–24)	20.6	14.9
Women		
Unemployment rate	13.0	11.9
Youth unemployment rate (14–24)	24.3	20.1

Source:　Commission of the EC (1990a) *Employment in Europe*, p. 33.

Although women represent over half of the unemployed in the EC, their unemployment differs from men's in several ways. Women are more likely to be unemployed as a result of wanting to re-enter the labour market. Official statistics also underestimate the number of women who would define themselves as actively seeking work, whereas men are more likely to be unemployed as a result of job loss or redundancy. Figure 2.2 shows that a higher proportion of women than men seek employment after a period of inactivity. Lack of childcare is one factor that makes it harder for women to find suitable work, as is the more limited range of jobs that are available to women.

Regional variations in employment opportunities can affect and restrict women's access to the labour market. As a result there are wide variations in rates of women's unemployment both within and between EC countries. Rates of unemployment differ for women in the 12 member states of the EC. They range from a rate of 25 per cent for women in Spain, to rates of under 10 per cent for women in Denmark, Germany, Luxembourg, the UK and Portugal. In Italy, for instance, women's rates of unemployment are twice those of men. For young women unemployment rates are significantly higher than for young men.

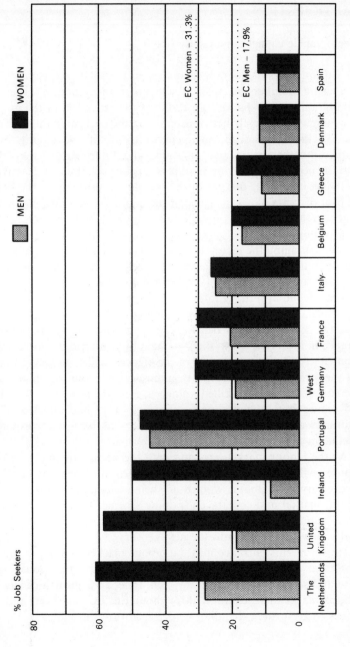

Figure 2.2   Percentage of women, compared to men, seeking jobs after a period of inactivity

Source: Commission of the EC (1989a) *Employment in Europe*.

FACTORS AFFECTING WOMEN'S LABOUR MARKET PARTICIPATION

Demographic changes and family size

As Europe faces demographic changes in the 1990s it is expected that increasing numbers of women will enter the labour market. The demographic 'time bomb' is a result of the reduction in the numbers of young economically active people and the corresponding ageing of the workforce. Indeed, the general trend of the ageing of the population throws up new questions about the care of the elderly, and the need for increasing resources for the economically inactive. By 2025 just under one quarter of the population throughout the EC will be over 65 years old. The ageing of the population, in turn, has led to a much greater reliance on women's unpaid labour to care for the elderly population at a time when several countries in the EC are also encouraging the increased labour market participation of women. These conflicts of interest in policy, which are particularly marked in the UK, are also evident in some other EC countries.

The decline in fertility rates throughout Europe has led the French and Belgian governments to encourage women to have larger families through generous family benefits. The concerns about fertility rates in France in the 1980s led to the statement by Mitterrand that increasing women's fertility rates was one of the biggest challenges facing Europe. At the same time France and Belgium are also countries that require increasing numbers of skilled women to enter the labour market. Table 2.5 shows how the decline in the birth rate has affected all EC countries and Table 2.6 shows that there has been a corresponding decline in the number of children per woman.

As the labour market ages and with the decline in young entrants, women will become a much larger proportion of new workers. As a reserve army of labour, women are being encouraged to re-enter the labour market and embark on training schemes to update their skills. As a result the number of economically active women aged 45 years and over will increase into the next century.

However, this entrance into the labour market is often in areas of work that continue to be segregated from the more prestigious, higher-paid and skilled jobs occupied by men. Indeed the growth of women's labour market participation throughout the EC has been and continues to be in the expanding service sector, not in industry.

Table 2.5   Birth rate per 1000 population, 1960 and 1986

	1960	1986
Belgium	17.0	11.9
Denmark	16.6	10.8
W. Germany	17.4	10.3
Greece	18.9	11.3
Spain	21.7	12.1 (1984)
France	17.9	14.1
Ireland	21.4	17.3
Italy	18.1	9.7
Luxembourg	15.9	11.7
The Netherlands	20.8	12.7
Portugal	23.9	12.4
UK	17.5	13.1

Source: Eurostat, Demographic Statistics 1988, Table VI.

Table 2.6   Number of children per woman (total period fertility rate)*, 1960 and 1986

	1960	1985 or 1986
Belgium	2.58	1.59[1]
Denmark	2.54	1.58
W. Germany	2.37	1.28
Greece	2.28	1.68
Spain	2.86	1.94[2]
France	2.73	1.84
Ireland	3.76	2.44
Italy	2.41	1.41
Luxembourg	2.28	1.45
The Netherlands	3.11	1.55
Portugal	3.01	1.63
UK	2.69[3]	1.78

* TPFR = average number of children who would be born per woman if women experienced the fertility rates specific to different age groups during the year in question throughout their childbearing lifespan.
[1] 1984
[2] 1982
[3] Great Britain

Source: Eurostat, Demographic Statistics 1988, Table VI and Table 9, col. 10.

Childcare

European labour markets continue to assume that the model of the 'typical' worker is one that engages in full-time, uninterrupted and continuous employment. As a result little consideration is given to the ways in which the labour market restricts women's employment opportunities because of their responsibilities to care not just for children but also for elderly, sick and disabled friends and relatives.

Lack of childcare has remained a major obstacle for women's labour market participation in all EC countries. It affects women's decisions about the type of work they can embark on, whether this be full-time work, part-time work or homeworking. Women's access to the labour market varies in the EC and is related to differing levels of childcare and employment rights, the structure of the labour market, levels of poverty and the economic necessity to work, as well as to general attitudes to women's labour market participation. Welfare programmes and social policies in different EC countries have a direct impact on women's access to paid employment. The discussion on different models of welfare, outlined in the previous chapter, was able to demonstrate the ways in which social policy can either encourage and promote women or place barriers to prevent them from entering the labour market. According to Phillips and Moss (1988) in the European Network on Childcare report, throughout the EC:

> the conditions under which men and women supply their labour to the labour market are not equal . . . this inequality is neither inherent or inevitable, but is socially determined. Wage rates and occupational position are not determined purely by market forces, but by the social costs of reproduction that are unequally distributed. A vicious circle operates: lack of power within the market place reinforces powerlessness within the home and in the political arena which, in turn, feeds back into the labour market. (p. 2)

Indeed, evidence from each member country of the EC shows a remarkable similarity in the expectations placed on women to care for children, even when they were also engaged in paid work. The European Network on Childcare found that the time spent by men and fathers on childcare and housework has not increased as more women have entered the labour market. It found, for instance, that in Italy 'men spent 6.3 hours a week where their wife had a job and 6.1 where she was not employed'. In The Netherlands, in families with children under 4 years old, 'fathers took no part in childcare, or only occasionally'. In Germany 92 per cent of men 'don't feel affected by housework. Little wonder since they do next to nothing . . . fathers have a kind of guest-role with their children'. It was only in Denmark that 'a high degree of joint responsibility towards the children' was reported (Phillips and Moss, 1988, p. 4).

It is the availablity of childcare that particularly affects the labour market participation of mothers with children under the age of 5. Patterns of labour market participation for women in this group vary within the EC. In Denmark, over 70 per cent of mothers are employed, compared to 55 per cent in Belgium and France, 30–40 per cent in Spain, Portugal, Greece and Luxembourg, and less than 30 per cent in the UK, Ireland, and The Netherlands. In contrast to Denmark, women in the latter band of countries are encouraged to stay at home to care for children and in the UK and The Netherlands, more than half of these women work less than 19 hours a week. Once children have started in school, women's labour market participation increases for women in the UK, whereas in some EC countries regional variations in employment are more likely to affect women's entry into paid employment. Figure 2.3 shows the activity rates of women with and without children in the member states.

The organisation, funding and levels of state support for childcare differ between and within EC countries. Figure 2.4 shows that the share of young children looked after by public childcare provision varies from one member state to another. The highest levels of publicly funded childcare are in Denmark, Italy and France and lowest in the UK and Portugal. Although some EC countries have better provision than others, there is a general belief of 'widespread unmet need', particularly in the services for children under 3 years old and in after-school care. According to Phillips and Moss (1988):

> The single biggest childcare problem in the Common Market is simply the lack of it. Most European working parents cannot choose to go out to work in the secure knowledge that their children will be well cared for. (p. 15)

Parental leave and maternity leave

Women's participation in the labour market is also affected by labour market and social policies that give entitlements for women to leave the labour market temporarily without loss of jobs, seniority and other

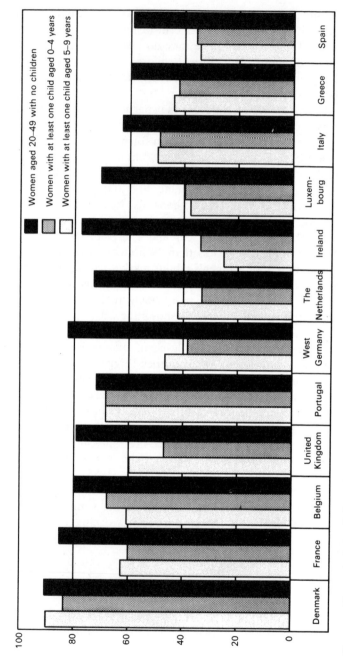

Figure 2.3 Activity rates of women with and without children in the member states, 1988

Women aged 20–49 with no children
Women with at least one child aged 0–4 years
Women with at least one child aged 5–9 years

Source: Commission of the EC (1989a) *Employment in Europe*.

Figure 2.4 Share of young children accommodated by public childcare provision in the member states, 1985 and 1988

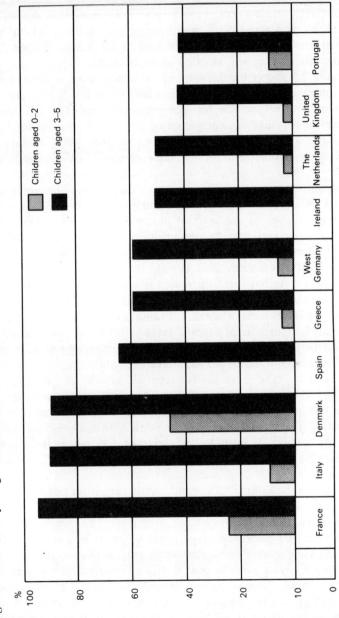

Source: Commission of the EC (1989a) *Employment in Europe*.

contractural arrangements. There is a wide variation in the entitlements to such policies that include parental leave and maternity leave. These policies have a crucial role to play in ensuring that women have continuity and security of employment and without which many women are left in vulnerable positions in the labour market. They are directly tied up with equality of opportunity.

Figure 2.5 shows the duration of maternity leave in each member state and the extent of compensation for lost wages. It is evident that there is a wide variation between member states. The UK has the lowest level of leave and compensation and this is compounded by the requirement of two years of full-time or five years of part-time continuous employment for the same employer before entitlements begin.

Parental leave entitles either women or men to take time out of work to care for a newborn baby, a sick child and in some cases a sick or disabled relative. At the heart of parental leave is the acknowledgement that parents have a responsibility for the care of children. Equally important is that employers need to recognise that parental duties do not stop when work begins.

Parental leave has been introduced in six EC countries and enables either the mother or father to take paid leave to care for a child at the end of maternity leave. Denmark, France, Greece, Italy, Portugal and Germany had introduced parental leave by 1989 and Luxembourg and The Netherlands were discussing the introduction of new schemes in 1990. Although there are no parental leave entitlements in Belgium, it is possible to take leave for between six months and one year for 'family and personal reasons'. Likewise in Spain, there is no parental leave but parents are able to get preferential treatment for job vacancies if they are returning to work within three years of the birth of a child. It is in Ireland and the UK where there are no parental leave or other related schemes either in operation or under discussion.

Table 2.7 shows how these entitlements vary from one EC country to another. The amount of time given for leave varies from ten weeks in Denmark to two years in France. However, in France, in firms with fewer than 100 employees, it is possible for an employer to refuse leave. In Greece leave entitlements only exist in the private sector and in firms employing over 100 people. Not all countries give payment for parental leave. Parental leave payments in Denmark are earnings-related at up to a maximum of 90 per cent of earnings, in Italy at only 30 per cent of earnings, while in France payment is only given where

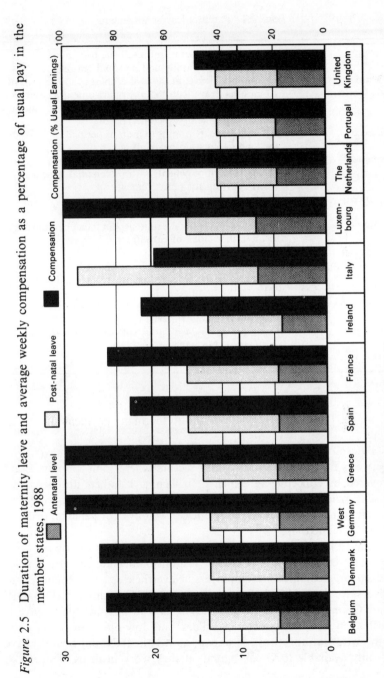

Figure 2.5 Duration of maternity leave and average weekly compensation as a percentage of usual pay in the member states, 1988

Source: Commission of the EC (1989a) *Employment in Europe.*

Table 2.7   Parental leave entitlements

Belgium	No leave entitlement, but a scheme for 'career interruption for family and personal reasons'.
Denmark	2½ months' leave, at 90% of earnings
W. Germany	10 months' leave, can be taken part-time if agreed with employer. Payment is flat-rate until the child is 6 months old, then payment is income related.
Greece	Parental leave: 6 months (3 months per parent, 6 months for lone parent), no payment.
Spain	No leave entitlement, but employees may take 3 years break from employment, with preferential treatment when applying for reinstatement.
France	24 months leave, can be taken part-time. No payment, unless 3 + children.
Italy	6 months' leave, for the mother, but it can be transferred to the father; 30% of earnings.
Ireland	No leave entitlement.
Luxembourg	No leave entitlement, but Government has proposed a scheme of parental leave lasting until a child is 2 years old.
The Netherlands	No leave entitlement, but Government proposed a scheme for 1988/9 for part-time leave.
Portugal	Leave for up to 24 months, with separate part-time entitlement. No payment.
UK	No leave entitlement.

there are three or more children and in Germany payment is at a flat rate.

Paternity leave, given to men at the birth of a child, also varies between EC countries and within sectors where some employees are covered by collective agreements. In Denmark fathers are given two weeks' paid leave, while in France only three days' leave is allowed. In several other countries leave for one or two days 'for personal reasons' can be claimed.

The responsibilities for children do not magically disappear when parents return to work. Parental responsibilities are rarely acknowledged or recognised by employers. Nevertheless, some countries do give statutory rights for parents to care for sick children. Denmark and Germany provide for paid leave, and in Portugal paid leave is restricted to public-sector workers and low-paid single parents, otherwise statutory leave is unpaid as it is in Italy and Spain. Leave is only available to Greek parents if they work in firms of over 100 employees. Although there are no statutory entitlements in the UK, Ireland, France, Belgium, Luxembourg or The Netherlands, collective agreements have established entitlements in some sectors.

Entitlements to parental leave and leave for family reasons clearly interact with the extent of childcare available for the young child. Given that it is in the provision of childcare for young children under the age of 3 years that a large gap exists, entitlements to leave play a vital and necessary role for the job security and continuity of employment of many women in the EC. In the UK and Ireland this continuity of employment is threatened by the lack of both parental leave entitlements and inadequate childcare for young children.

'Flexible' work patterns

In recognition of the fact that many women who embark on part-time work after the birth of a child re-enter the labour market for lower-paid and lower-skilled jobs, several EC countries have given parents the right to choose flexibility at work by reducing working hours. Introducing flexible working arrangements prevents the situation arising where women are forced to leave their jobs and re-enter the labour market for lower-status part-time work.

Some of this flexibility to move into part-time work or reduce working hours is covered under parental leave arrangements. For instance, it is possible for French and German parents to work part-time, rather than take the whole period of leave off, although in Germany this is subject to the employers' approval. The Dutch scheme enables both parents to work a reduced week of 20 hours for six months, to be taken any time until the child is 2 years old. Workers in the public sector in Luxembourg and civil servants in Germany who have children have the right to work a shorter day. Although Spanish and Portuguese parents with young children have some rights to a shorter working day, in reality working practices have made it very difficult for parents to take up these opportunities.

The absence of legislation in the UK has to led to several cases under the Sex Discrimination Act that establish the precedent that women are able to return to their jobs on a part-time basis after the birth of a child. Increasing numbers of women in the UK are embarking on job-share schemes that provide all of the benefits of full-time work, with the flexibility of part-time work. Here two women are employed on a full-time contract but share the job half-time. Increasingly employers are looking at more flexible ways of working;

sometimes these are to the benefit of the parent and enable choice in working hours and working times.

Many of the schemes that exist for flexible and reduced working hours, for moving from full-time to part-time work and job-sharing give a greater level of protection and flexibility for women working in professional, skilled and public sector jobs. For the women who make up the large unskilled, low-paid, and unprotected workforce, often in the private sector, where the only opportunities for working are in temporary, non-contractual jobs, such schemes do not touch them. It is for these women that the concept of flexibility frequently takes another meaning. Flexibility can also be a means of exploiting women's lack of choices in the labour market for the changing needs and requirements of employers. Instead of offering contracts of permanent and regular employment, employers are able to use women as a reserve army of labour, hiring and firing them when it suits their demand for labour. This is a million miles away from providing women with the flexibility to arrange their working hours around their child care commitments. Inevitably it is the women with the least bargaining power, with the lowest skills, pay and status, who are most vulnerable to employers' requirements for flexible labour.

Lone parenthood

The lack of childcare throughout the EC exacerbates the opportunities for seeking paid work for the growing numbers of lone parents in all EC countries. The lack of a standardised definition of what constitutes lone parenthood makes it difficult to assess the number of single-parent families in the EC. However, some attempts have been made to develop a standard definition at the EC level, to define lone parents as people who do not live in a couple, but who may or may not live with other adults, and living with at least one child under 18 years old. Table 2.8 gives a tentative estimate on the number of lone parents as a proportion of all families with children.

Further statistical evidence of lone-parent households as a percentage of the population can be found in the 1987 European Omnibus Survey special supplement, based on a sample of 23 234 Europeans aged over 15 years. Table 2.9 shows that as a percentage of the population the highest numbers of lone-parent households are found in Belgium and the UK, while the lowest numbers are found in Ireland and Greece.

Table 2.8   Lone-parent families as a proportion of all families with children

14%	Denmark, UK
12–13%	Germany, France
10–12%	Belgium, Luxembourg, The Netherlands
5–10%	Spain, Ireland, Portugal
Under 5%	Greece

Source: Commission of the EC (1989c) *Lone Parent Families in the European Community*, Report for the Commission by the Family Policy Studies Centre, p. 51

Table 2.9   Lone-parent households, 1987

	% of population
Belgium	7.2
Denmark	4.5
W. Germany	4.6
Greece	2.6
Spain	4.8
France	4.7
Ireland	3.3
Italy	4.7
Luxembourg	4.0
The Netherlands	5.2
Portugal	3.7
UK	6.1

Source: Commission of the EC (1987) *European Omnibus Survey.*

Despite the tentative nature of the estimates of lone parents in the EC, lone parents share a number of common characteristics throughout the EC. Most notable is that the majority of lone parents are women, ranging from 80 per cent in Belgium to 91 per cent in the UK. Lone parents are more likely to be divorced/separated than unmarried and to have fewer children than married couples. They are also likely to be over 25 years old and their children to be on average older than in two-parent families. The majority of lone parents live alone with their children.

Research from all EC countries has also shown that lone parents are more likely to experience poverty and have lower living standards than two-parent families. For instance, lone parents are more likely to live in substandard accommodation and are less likely to own a car or to have savings than two-parent families. In Belgium only 36 per cent of lone-parent families have savings compared to 65 per cent of two-parent families and 40 per cent have a car compared to 88 per cent of two-parent families. In the UK 30 per cent have a car compared with 85 per cent of two parent families.

The 1987 *European Omnibus Survey* showed that lone parents are likely to fall into the bottom quarter of the income distribution. However, the incomes of lone mothers are significantly lower than those of lone fathers. Employment is vitally important for many female-headed lone-parent families and there is a wide variation in employment rates for lone mothers between EC countries. When lone parents do work their average earnings are significantly lower than the average earnings of two parent families.

Table 2.10 shows that there is a wide variation in the extent to which lone mothers are in full-time and part-time work, or who are unemployed. For example, 63 per cent of lone mothers in Luxembourg and 50 per cent in Denmark work full-time compared to only 5 per cent in The Netherlands and 7 per cent in the UK, where a higher proportion of working lone mothers work part-time. Lone mothers are more likely to be out of the labour force in The Netherlands, Ireland and the UK. These figures correlate with the lower levels of childcare in these countries and a higher dependence on state (often means-tested) benefits.

Atypical working patterns

It is clear that the pattern of the male career path, of long, unbroken periods of continuous, full-time employment and geographical mobility does not fit into a woman's pattern of employment. A woman's employment career is likely to be broken up by childcare with a return to part-time or full-time employment later. The restructuring of the labour market in the 1980s and early 1990s, prompted by recession, led to a growth of atypical forms of employment. This includes part-time work, homeworking, casual and temporary work, seasonal work, agency work, on-call and non-contractual work. Atypical working patterns are becoming increasingly common, especially for married women and women with children, throughout the EC. Indeed, the growth of new jobs since the 1980s has largely been achieved through the creation of non-standard, atypical jobs, many of which have been temporary or part-time jobs. The price of this flexibility, which has

Table 2.10   Lone mothers[1] with children aged 0 to 4 years by labour force status, 1985

	In labour force			Out of labour force	Total[2]
	Employed		*Unemployed[4]*		
	full-time	*part-time[3]*			
Belgium	46	11	26	17	100
Denmark	50	17	15	19	100
W. Germany	27	14	14	45	100
Greece	38	9	11	42	100
France	44	8	21	27	100
Ireland	8	3	17	72	100
Italy	49	7	12	32	100
Luxembourg	63	8	8	22	100
The Netherlands	5	10	10	74	100
UK	7	10	14	69	100

[1] Lone mothers who live in the household of others are not included, but they do not exclude all those who are cohabiting or who have a temporarily absent spouse.

[2] Because of rounding and some 'no replies' the numbers shown in the table may not sum to 100 exactly.

[3] As defined by respondents. In practice the hours of 'part-time' work as defined in this way vary substantially from country to country. For example, in France, Italy, Denmark and Greece at least one in four of all mothers who work 'part-time' work 30 hours or more a week whereas in The Netherlands, the UK and Ireland, the proportion is less than 10 per cent.

[4] Those who, in the week before the survey, were actively seeking work (including some who were not for a number of specified reasons, for example, waiting for the results of a job application).

Source: Eurostat (1985) *Labour Force Survey* special analysis carried out by the EC Statistical Office at the request of Peter Moss, Thomas Coram Research Insitute, for the European Childcare Network.

coincided with the deregulation of employment in the UK, has been greater job insecurity, loss of employment protection, lower pay and associated benefits and reduced status at work. It inevitably provides flexibility for employers seeking to reduce labour costs but often makes women's employment choices more rigid, less secure and more vulnerable.

Part-time work

In 1987 28 per cent of women working in the EC worked part-time. This figure is higher for married women and for women aged between 50 and 64 years. Figure 2.6 shows part-time employment as a share of total employment in 1988. In all member states women's share of part-time work exceeds men's, and is the highest in The Netherlands, the UK and Denmark.

Evidence from all EC countries shows that women who work part-time are increasingly concentrated in the service sector, that they have low levels of education and training and are more frequently engaged on temporary rather than permanent contracts of employment (OECD, 1987). Combined with poorer job security, many part-time workers receive inadequate and often non-existent social security coverage.

The growth of part-time work has in part been a reflection of the changing nature of the labour market. The growth of the service sector, in particular, has led to a new demand for part-time workers, who are principally women. It has also been a reflection of the lower costs to employers who are likely to view women part-time workers as secondary workers. It has fitted into women's domestic routines and in the absence of alternative forms of childcare enables women to combine paid employment with childcare in a dual role. However, for many women part-time work is not voluntary, but arises because of domestic commitments. There is a strong correlation between the existence of young children and part-time work. More than half of the women who work part-time are over 30 years old and have young children.

Employment opportunities open to part-time employees tend to be limited in scope, being confined to the service sector and to industry where they are available in a narrow range of occupations, for example in food, textiles, clothing and footwear. Part-time workers are frequently concentrated into the lower semi-skilled and unskilled grades. They are likely to take a drop in skills and pay when moving from full-time work and be employed in jobs that underutilise their skills and qualifications. Moreover, they are likely to have few opportunities for promotion and career development and are more likely to work in small firms. In the UK one-half of women in part-time work are employed in firms employing fewer than 25 people.

Many part-time workers receive a lower hourly rate of pay than full-time workers. In most EC countries this is compounded by the

Figure 2.6   Part-time employment as a share of total employment in the member states, 1988

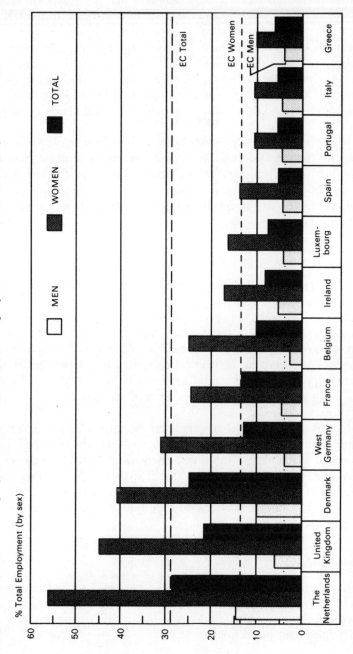

% Total Employment (by sex)

Source: Commission of the EC (1989a) *Employment in Europe*.

difficulties in making comparisons under equal pay legislation between female part-time workers and male full-time workers. In the UK, for instance, 'material difference' arguments have enabled employers to maintain differential rates of pay under the 1970 Equal Pay Act. However, little is known about the actual pay position of part-time workers, since the collection of official statistics throughout the EC does not provide figures on part-time workers whose earnings fall below tax thresholds, or whose earnings are not declared by employers.

Membership of trade unions is much lower for part-time workers than for full-time workers. Only about one out of every five part-time working women is a member of a trade union in the UK, and twice as many full-time working women as part-time women are in trade unions. Other EC countries reflect similar patterns of part-time membership.

Temporary work

Temporary work includes work on fixed-term contracts, agency work, casual work and seasonal work. Women are a rising group of temporary workers; however, statistics are rarely held on women temporary workers. In Italy, where records are kept, 49 per cent of temporary jobs were held by women in 1985. Figure 2.7 show that, on average, 11.7 per cent of women, compared to 9.4 per cent of men, were working under temporary contracts in 1988. Temporary work is more common in some of the poorer member states, including Spain, Portugal and Greece.

Increasing numbers of new jobs are being offered with temporary contracts and like part-time jobs they are often taken up out of lack of choice or availability of full-time or permanent work. Indeed over half of women workers in the EC stated that they took temporary work because of the absence of permanent work (Commission of the EC, 1990b). This was particularly the case for working women in Spain, Greece and Portugal.

Homeworking

Like part-time work, homeworking is almost exclusively female and is largely confined to manufacturing work. Homeworking is most usually characterised as work from home paid on piece rates, with no employment protection:

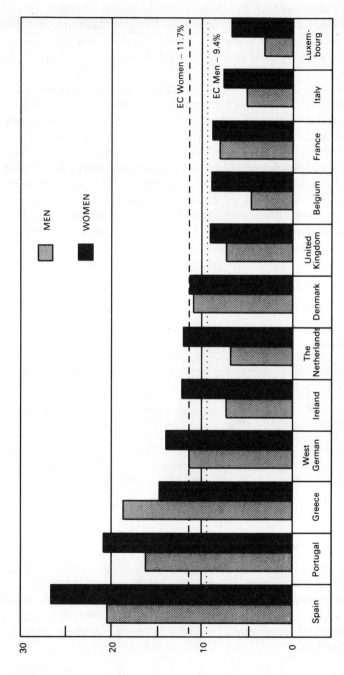

Figure 2.7 Share of employees working under temporary contracts in the member states, 1988

Source: Commission of the EC (1989a) *Employment in Europe.*

Homeworking provides a long-standing example of casualised employment, where there is no effective regulation of the suppliers and where the worker has no security, no rights and relatively, if not absolutely poor pay. (Allen and Wolkowitz, 1987, p. 8)

For these reasons the actual extent of homeworking is unknown. However, it has been estimated that there are over 300 000 homeworkers in the UK, the vast majority of whom are women and in particular women from minority ethnic groups (Bisset and Huws, 1984). It has also been estimated that there are 1.5 million homeworkers in Greece, Spain, Portugal and Italy. Rates of pay are notoriously low and highly exploitative and many women remain out of the reach of equal pay and other forms of protective legislation. Moreover, homeworking is widespread in the poorer peripheral regions of the EC, and in urban areas close to certain manufacturing industries, for example, textiles. Table 2.11 gives minimum estimates of homeworkers in a number of member states.

Table 2.11   Minimum estimates of homeworkers in selected member states

Country	Year	Number	Proportion of women %
Italy	1985	700 000	over 90
France	1985	59 600	82
Portugal	1983	50 000	over 90
Spain	1986	490 000	75
UK	1981	229 000	70
Greece	1986	225 000	over 90

Source: Commission of the EC (1989a) *Employment in Europe*, p. 90.

Unpaid family helpers

In several EC countries unpaid family helpers make up a significant group of working women. They include women working in family businesses or farms, with no contracts, employment protection or pay. Although the number of unpaid family helpers has declined, they represent 34 per cent of working women in Greece and 10 per cent in Spain.

The value of women's work

Pay is decisive in determining the social status of an individual, since the 'value' placed on an individual reflects the pay received. The greater the occupational segregation and number of women in an occupation, the greater the pay differential between men and women. The jobs that women perform and the jobs that men perform, even where equally productive, give a lower valuation to women's work, because the work is performed by women. This has an important bearing on women's pay and the way that skill is determined is central to an understanding of women's pay. It is clear that equal pay policies will have little success if women's work is deemed to be inferior, because it is women doing the work. This leads to a low valuation being placed on women's work. Familial ideology, the family wage and the ideological construction of the roles of women ensure that skill is a subjective concept:

> to suggest that the remarkable coincidence between women's labour and unskilled labour in our economy is solely the result of discriminatory training programmes, or even home responsibilities, is surely naive, since it implies that with educational upgrading and the provision of more day nurseries women would take their place alongside skilled men workers and gender-ghettoes would disappear. (Phillips and Taylor, 1980, p. 55)

The sexual division of labour and resulting lower pay scales for women is accepted, unquestioned and regarded as inevitable by male workers and employers alike.

Family ideology and the role of the state: the effects of social policies on the position of working women

It is clear that state policies have often neglected the specific needs of women and are often constructed in gender-neutral terms. The postwar years brought many new opportunities for women in terms of new job opportunities and the collective provision of welfare services. But they continued to view women within the context of family and marriage.

It is clear that the role of the state has brought with it many conflicting and often contradictory priorities, often as a result of deeply embedded ideologies relating to the role of women in the family and at work. Social policies have both a direct and an indirect effect on the extent to which women can participate in the labour market. For instance, the extent to which social policies facilitate the provision of childcare has an enormous effect on the extent to which women are able to work full-time or part-time and indeed work outside the home at all. For instance, in the UK the provision of day-care and nursery education has broad welfare functions, whereas in Denmark these functions are coupled with a desire to provide opportunities for women's employment outside the home. In the same way the provision of maternity leave, paternity leave and parental leave also affects the capacity of women to return to work after childbirth.

Family ideology, implicit in much family and welfare law and employment practices throughout the EC, plays a large part in restricting the position of women in the labour market. The importance attached to motherhood and women's roles in the home means that the highly exploited forms of atypical working are often the only choice women have for paid work, as a result of their responsibilities for children. Of particular relevance to women's pay are long-standing debates about the 'family wage' in countries like France and the UK. It has its roots in the rise of industrial capitalism and trade unionism which sought to remove women from the labour market and assert the dominance of male labour. Although the idea of a family wage is still strongly defended in several European countries, it is now considered to be in contravention of equal pay legislation. However, it has had the effect of maintaining an ideology that women's pay is supplementary to that provided by the male breadwinner, or sufficient to support a single woman with no dependants.

3 Women and the Single European Market

WHAT IS THE SINGLE EUROPEAN MARKET?

The 1986 Single European Act introduced 286 proposals designed to remove the physical, technical and fiscal barriers between EC member states. Its purpose is to take the Community towards a full common market through the completion of economic and monetary union. Abolishing the barriers to free movement of persons, services and capital will enable Europe to trade as one block in the world market, and compete with large and economically powerful countries like the USA and Japan. The Single European Act also recognised that economic and social cohesion would be strengthened by the completion of the internal market. But what is meant by economic and social cohesion and who is likely to benefit from it?

The end of 1992 was set as the date for the removal of the obstacles for the internal market. In the run up to 1992 the plans to remove the physical and technical barriers to trade were well developed. However, the more politically controversial areas relating to the 'social dimension' of the internal market have been slow to reach the decision-making table in the EC.

This chapter will discuss how the Single European Market could affect women. It will look at the various ways in which the position of women in the labour market will be affected by growing competition in an internal market. Readers interested in how the Community is responding to women's specific needs in the internal market through policy initiatives should turn to Chapter 6.

WOMEN'S EMPLOYMENT AND THE SINGLE EUROPEAN MARKET

It is not easy to make firm predictions of the impact of the internal market on women. The Van Hemeldonck Report for the Women's Committee of the European Parliament (1988) stated that 'the lack of indicators describing the reality of women's lives in EEC and Member

41

States' statistics makes it difficult to forecast what changes will occur after 1992' (p. 5). Nevertheless, the previous chapter provided a number of indicators of the employment position of women, from which it is possible to make some tentative assessments of the impact of the single market on women. The Commission's 1989 and 1990 *Employment in Europe* reports (1989a, 1990a) and the report by Pauline Conroy-Jackson for the Commission's Equal Opportunities Unit (Commission of the EC, 1990b), in addition to the Van Hemeldonck Report, give good initial indicators of the effect of the single market on women.

The single market will profoundly change women's employment in the EC in both the medium term and the long term. There is, however, no agreement about the pace of change or the timescale involved. The Commission has argued that employment growth will be an inevitable outcome of new forms of economic growth and competition and has conducted a number of preliminary studies on the sectoral and regional impact of the market.

However, this positive benefit will not be evenly felt. What does this mean for women? Are women going to benefit from these new forms of competition and cohesion? How will it affect the already vulnerable position women occupy in the labour market? The last chapter showed that despite the growing demand for women's participation in the labour market, women start from a weaker position than men. Their employment is restricted by rigid labour markets that fail to provide social, employment and training programmes that enable their full integration into work. This information is crucial for understanding how women start from a weaker position *vis-à-vis* men and in predicting the likely effects of the single market on women. According to a report by the European Parliament's Social Affairs Committee the:

> existing forms of segregation, discrimination and unequal opportu-
> nities for women in the labour market make women particularly
> vulnerable to adverse effects in the completion of the internal
> market, for example job losses, and increase in types of work
> without social protection and an increasing demand for flexibility
> and excessively long working days in certain regions, thereby
> increasing the number of women living in poverty. (European
> Parliament, 1990a, pp. 6–7)

The bulk of the Commission's work relating to the sectoral and regional impact of the internal market has failed to recognise the specific effect this will have on women. Not surprisingly women were never intended to be the main beneficiaries of greater prosperity in Europe. Nor were women singled out as a group facing particular disadvantages. Both the Padoa-Schioppa Report (1987) on the economic repercussions of the European Internal Market and the Cecchini Report (1988) on the cost of non-Europe fail to mention women.

The 1988 Cecchini Report on the cost of non-Europe was the first attempt by the EC to predict the effects of the removal of trade barriers on the EC as a whole. The report was based on a series of research studies, published in 16 volumes. It optimistically predicted that up to five million new jobs could be created, with some short-term job losses. Cecchini argued that the removal of technical, physical and fiscal barriers would reduce costs to industry. This would lead to 500 000 new jobs in the first year and a further 1.8 million new jobs within six years. However, this would take its toll on inefficient producers who would be priced out of the market by greater economies of scale, restructuring and more competition. Interestingly, Cecchini found that governments would benefit from savings in costs and that this would lead to economic expansion and the creation of five million new jobs.

However, many critiques have been made of the report, and its findings are now largely seen as over-optimistic. In a report commissioned by the Labour Group of the European Parliament, Henry Neuberger (1989) argues that internal market measures would only create one million jobs over six years, with more job losses than predicted by Cecchini in the first three years. Neuberger rightly argues that it is unrealistic and unreasonable to separate the economic and social dimensions of the internal market.

Gains will be felt by some women in some regions, industries or sectors of the EC, but losses will also significantly affect other women working in some of the more sensitive and vulnerable regions and sectors of industry in the EC. The Chair of the European Parliament's Women's Committee, Christine Crawley, believes that the prospects for women in the single market herald both 'good news and bad news' (interview, Strasbourg, 12 September 1990). The good news is that the lifting of trade restrictions coincides with a demographic upheaval, referred to in the last chapter. This will provide more opportunities for women who have qualifications, skills, access to good training and retraining programmes and who have good childcare support. As a result women could have more choices than ever before. There will be more opportunities for women to enter skilled work at a managerial level. Although increases in employment opportunities for women exist, they may not necessarily be in the areas where women have acquired new skills.

The bad news is that there are real dangers that many of the sectors where women have traditionally worked will be squeezed out by fiercer competition. Employers will be forced to change patterns of work and these will play on women's already vulnerable positions in the labour market. The growth of atypical working patterns will disproportionately affect women. Indeed, the expansion of the service sector will continue well into the next century to provide new points of access for women into the labour market. However, many of these new jobs have been and will continue to be part-time or temporary. The quality, protection and desirability of these new forms of jobs are questionable and they will not necessarily be created in the areas where there is a decline in industrial jobs.

Unless these developments are matched by targeting resources into good quality training for women and better forms of protection, then the increased competition for the single market will further distort women's vulnerable position. At a regional level women who live in the poorer and more peripheral regions of the EC will be further disadvantaged. An analysis of the main sectors of employment in which women are engaged will provide a picture of where women are most vulnerable.

The scenario of employment patterns in Europe is one of concentrations of highly skilled labour in core areas of the EC, sometimes referred to as a 'golden triangle'. Industrial and technological design, innovation and production, as well as research and development, are likely to be increasingly concentrated in the Euro-centre or the golden triangle of the EC. Included in the golden triangle are northern Italy, Germany, France, the Benelux countries and south-east England. Doubts do exist about the inclusion of south-east England in the core area of development without greater levels of investment in transport, training and industry. It is in this core area that industry is modernising and developing. Here employers have requirements for technological skills, where good conditions of employment with high levels of pay and associated benefits are offered.

Beyond this core there will be a new outer fringe of industrial development mainly for the production of bulk consumer goods, with lower levels of pay and skill. It is here, in this outer fringe, that multinational companies will play a significant role in pooling the local labour force at relatively low wages. It will provide employment for the production of goods for the immediate market or to be imported into the core. Although there will not be a significant demand for skilled labour, in the long term this sector would suffer from a lack of product development (confined to the core area). The other side of the coin is that there will be greater concentrations of unskilled labour, unemployment and underemployment in particular regions or the outer core areas. There is a real danger that the traditional sectors of women's employment will be squeezed out by fiercer competition. Changing working patterns will also affect the vulnerable position of women in the labour market and the growth of atypical working patterns will disproportionately affect women, particularly in the poorer and more peripheral regions of the EC. As a result there is a need to target resources into women's training and better forms of protection for women, including childcare, especially in these more vulnerable areas.

The impact of the single market on different sectors and regions is dependent on a number of factors that will either open up new forms of competition or squeeze some firms out of the market. These include:

- whether protection has existed in the past, for instance, through non-tariff barriers (for example, differing technical standards and regulations, administrative barriers, differences in Value Added Taxation, government procurement restrictions);
- the possibilities existing for economies of scale and mergers to remain competitive;
- how far producers in different sectors and regions can remain competitive with the opening up of markets (as a result of the removal of frontiers);
- the extent of good communications (including transport) to enable some areas and regions to take advantage of new markets;
- whether certain sectors or regions have highly skilled workers adaptable to new markets;
- the degree of concentration of certain sectors.

Growing competition will be a direct effect of the internal market. This will lead to restructuring and relocation, closure, take overs and mergers as companies make adjustments for the single market. For some sectors this will mean closure and job losses as firms are priced out of the market. For others this will lead to take-overs and mergers to ensure survival as companies seek European rather than national status. There will be a particularly regional effect to these changes, for instance, for women in the food industry and clothing and textiles. It is expected, therefore, that employment growth in the single market will not be evident in some areas and regions of the EC.

Thus while the Single European Market may create new employment opportunities, it is also potentially hazardous for women. Traditional areas of women's employment are facing restructuring, but unless this restructuring takes account of women's economic and social position there are dangers that women could lose out significantly on the benefits anticipated from the internal market. New job opportunities alone will be insufficient to ensure that women will achieve equality with men in the labour market. According to Pauline Conroy-Jackson (1990):

> The completion of the Internal Market is no micro-wave oven that will irradiate away inequality like a bad germ. If the ingredients of women's position on the labour market are spoiled or distorted, inequality will merely be exacerbated. (p. 29)

Industry

The single market is likely to have the most significant impact in industry. Fiercer competition and more economies of scale will be an inevitable result of the removal of trade barriers. Indeed, half of all employment in industry is in sectors that are potentially sensitive to the single market. Many of these are labour intensive industries that employ large numbers of women.

The EC Commission's *Employment in Europe* report (1989a) groups four main areas of industrial employment that are sensitive to restructuring. These include industries that are competitively weak (high-tech equipment), industries facing rationalisation (including pharmaceuticals and drinks), industries liable to some rationalisation (including confectionery, pasta and electrical equipment) and industries where distribution networks may change (including textiles, shoes and toys).

Within these four areas the Commission identifies 40 sectors of industrial employment in the EC that are sensitive to restructuring and job lossess. In nine of the most sensitive branches of industry women represent more than 45 per cent of employees. These are also jobs with low wage costs. They include clothing, household textiles, footwear, toys and sports goods, photographic equipment, cocoa, chocolate, sugar, cotton, jewellery and pharmaceutical goods. In a further nine industries women represent between 30 per cent and 45 per cent of employees. These industries include radio/TV, electrical lighting, wool, medical equipment, telecommunications, electrical appliances, ceramics, carpets and pasta. Although women represent a smaller proportion of employeees in the other sensitive industries, they are clustered in manual and assembly-line jobs that will be vulnerable to restructuring. Figure 3.1 shows the share of female employment in four main sectors of sensitive industrial employment.

There will also be a regional effect to this. In the poorer southern European countries and parts of Italy and the UK a much larger proportion of the female labour force is employed in the sensitive industries. Like clothing and textiles, many of these industries have been highly protected. In Greece and Portugal, nearly half of all industrial employment is located in labour intensive manufacturing industries like textiles, clothing, footwear and food processing. The more prosperous northern European countries will not be as disadvantaged as the southern European countries since they have a more competitive industrial base and strong industries. However, in Ireland over half the employment is in competitively strong sectors. This is a reflection of the strong presence of multinational companies specialising in high-tech production and pharmaceutical goods which are very competitive. In comparison the UK ranks alongside Spain and Greece in its share of traditional, declining or slow-growth industries. These are also countries where industrial decline has not been matched by the growth of high-tech industries evident in the other northern European countries.

To avoid these disparities becoming even more enhanced in the single market, and having a disproportionate effect on women, there is a very real need for strong industrial and labour market policies to ensure that all sectors are able to be competitive in the single market. This is perhaps most evident in the textile and clothing industry.

Textiles and clothing

Since the 1970s the textiles and clothing industry has faced decline and restructuring in most EC countries, especially Germany, the UK, Ireland, The Netherlands and France. This has been the result of reduced domestic demand for textiles and clothing and growing

Figure 3.1 Share of female employment in sensitive sectors, 1986

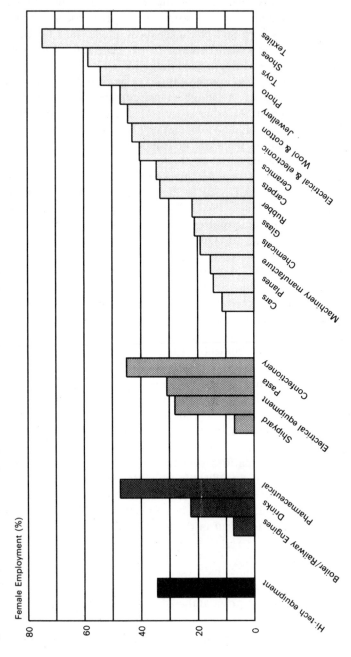

Source: Commission of the EC (1989a) *Employment in Europe.*

international competition in the industry from developing and newly industrialised countries.

The ending of the GATT Multifibre Agreements-IV in 1992 will profoundly affect the textiles and clothing sectors throughout the EC, by opening up competition, especially from low-wage countries both inside and outside the EC. Clothing and textiles throughout the EC are highly feminised. For example, women represent 75 per cent of all employees in textiles in the EC. Many are unskilled and low-paid. They will be affected by growing competition as employers seek to reduce labour costs and increase production. As a result there will be an enormous amount of restructuring of employment through job losses and more atypical forms of employment, for instance, home-working, subcontracting and temporary work.

In the Commission's report (1989b) on the costs of non-europe in textiles and clothing, it is predicted that there will be an increase in the use of subcontracting on an international scale and a move to more decentralised and fragmented production. In attempts to reduce labour costs there is an increasing likelihood of relocation to the low-wage areas of the EC. In the same way that lower labour costs in third world countries priced out many European competitors in the 1970s and 1980s, relocation to poorer EC countries could create a shift in production from high wage to low-wage economies. Growing international competition and the ending of the Multifibre Agreements are likely to enhance this trend not just on a European scale but on a global scale. For these reasons textiles and clothing will be one area of industry where women will face significant job losses in the single market:

> Employment in clothing and textiles will continue to decline in the European Community in existing enterprises and firms, generating a pool of redundant and unemployed women poorly equipped for employment in other branches of industry. (Commission of the EC, 1990b, p. 35)

In Italy, textiles and clothing have been a vital source of employment for women. Ten per cent of women work in the textile and clothing industry, within which certain sectors are highly feminised, for instance knitwear and clothing. The importance of textiles and clothing can be shown from Italy's prominence in exports. In 1987 Italy was the largest exporter of clothes in the industrial world and the second largest exporter of textiles. However, Italy has held onto its relatively strong position by fragmenting production. This will become all the more important with growing international competition in the single market. The inevitable result of the fragmentation of production is that more women will work in the hidden black economy, in unregulated and atypical forms of employment, where they will have little job security, lower pay and little or no social protection.

The decline of the textile and clothing industry in Germany, coupled with restructuring, has led to significant job losses since the 1960s. Women have always been a large proportion of employees in the industry, representing 80 per cent of those working in the clothing industry. They have worked in the jobs that were more vulnerable to restructuring and have particularly suffered from job losses. Germany, like other northern European countries, has responded to growing international competition by restructuring the industry, introducing more automation and technology, and shifting to more specialised, upmarket products.

In order to avoid the enormous problems faced by the restructuring of textiles and clothing, in the light of growing international competition and the single market, there is a need for a wide range of policies to protect women from unemployment and exploitation. These include reconversion and retraining programmes for women, particularly in regions where textiles and clothing has been the major source of employment and where women lack the skills or the opportunities to enter new forms of employment. Of particular and growing importance is that women have access to legal and social protection against exploitation of their labour.

Electronics

The electronics industry is a large and growing employer of women throughout the EC. However, there is a high level of sex segregation within the industry where women account for the majority of 'unskilled' or 'semi-skilled' assembly line operators, while the technical and professional activities are largely dominated by men. In the electronics industry, like the textiles and electrical engineering industries, there is a move to much greater domination by men as technological advances in the northern European countries require highly skilled labour. In contrast the poorer newly-industrialised countries, for example Portugal, Spain and Greece, are increasingly taking over the unskilled or semi-skilled production of components and goods (Willoughby, 1990)

Service sectors

While it is anticipated that the single market will see a significant rise in service sector employment, particularly for women, it too will face restructuring from the removal of internal barriers and the former protection of national markets. The Commission's 1989 *Employment in Europe* report states that there will be increasing polarisation of service sector jobs between those that are low-paid and low-skilled and those that are high-paid and high-skilled. Indeed it is likely that women will be forced into low-paid and low-skilled jobs.

Little is known about the pay and employment position of women in the services. For a variety of reasons, including the difficulty in placing a productive value on service sector employment, few statistics are collected. The EC statistical office has a wealth of statistical information on the position on women in industry, but a dearth of information on women in the services. This is particularly important since service sector employment is taking up a growing proportion of all female labour. Within the service sector there are likely to be specific changes taking place with the completion of the internal market.

Public sector employment

One obvious and direct effect will be the opening up of a significant number of civil service posts to citizens of other EC countries. This will provide more opportunities to work in other countries. Women make up a large proportion of public servants in several EC countries: 80 per cent in Denmark, 41 per cent in France, 36 per cent in Belgium and 30 per cent in Denmark. However, women are less likely than men to be mobile. The constraints of childcare, family and domestic responsibilities and commitments will mean that fewer women than men will be able to take up these opportunities in other EC countries. Moreover, the developments taking place in other areas of service sector employment mean that women are more likely to be squeezed out of their traditional low-skilled jobs in this sector by new technology.

Women are also heavily concentrated in the welfare sectors. For example, in France women represent about 60 per cent of employees in the health and education sectors. Through the mutual recognition of qualifications and diplomas throughout the EC, freedom of movement will be equally open to men and women in these sectors. Moreover as more women re-enter the labour market, there is likely to be a growth in the demand for childcare and domestic services. Although the Commission does identify an increase in unskilled and manual work in areas such as tourism, hotel and catering, and domestic and childcare services, these will reinforce women's existing segregation in the labour market. Moreover, the growth of these sectors will not automatically provide alternative employment for women in regions of the EC facing restructuring.

Telecommunications, transport, business services, and banking and finance will also face changes through the opening up of markets.

Business services

Business services will be affected by the opening up of new markets. They will have significant growth potential, brought about by an increasing demand for services, often of a specialist nature. These include translating, legal, financial, computing, public relations, communications, management consultancy, property and other re-lated services. They will often be services contracted out to specialist firms and it is likely that there will be an increase in small or medium sized companies providing these services in the future. This could be advantageous to skilled women, particularly in the light of the trend of more women setting up small companies throughout the EC. How-ever, they do place a high demand on skills acquisition where women have a disproportionate access to education and skills training than men. Likewise the predicted growth in the service and leisure industries will also open up increased job opportunities for skilled women. For many unskilled women displaced by increasing competi-tion and restructuring in industry, the growth of these sectors will offer few opportunities unless there is a major injection of resources for women's training.

Banking and financial services

As shown in the previous chapter women make up a very large proportion of employees in the banking and finance sector, the majority of whom are in lower-skilled and lower-paid occupations. The Commission's 1988 study *The 'Costs of Non-Europe' in Financial Services* fails to predict the employment effects of financial liberal-isation in the single market. The single market is set to bring with it a massive expansion of financial activity with a corresponding increase in the competition for banking services and products. Despite this increased activity, there is no clear indication of a growth in employment opportunities, rather that this growth will be met by new forms of technology, such as electronic banking. These new banking methods do threaten job losses for women in the lower-skilled and clerical occupations where women can be displaced by new technology. Rationalisation of banking will also lead to the need for more skilled workers. It has been shown that women have lower skills than men in this sector and will correspondingly have lower access to the new skilled jobs in the future.

The UK is likely to see substantial restructuring in banking. Although women represent the large majority of employees in banking and finance in the UK, 90 per cent of women work in the lower-paid, white-collar jobs in clerical and related occupations. This is compared to less than 4 per cent of women in management, largely working in traditional female areas of employment such as personnel and administration. Women are increasingly being targeted by the banks and financial houses for future employment, recruitment and retention. Correspondingly, the banks have begun to respond by recognising that women need help in remaining at work or in taking up new job opportunities, for instance, through childcare provision in workplace nurseries, career break schemes and flexible working. According to Ivy Cameron (1990) of the banking union, BIFU, these enticements have been largely 'superficial' given the major restructuring and reorganisation of banking and finance which is reinforcing low pay and job segregation. For instance, banking and finance is fast moving in the direction of 24 hour operation, particularly through regional and 'geographically inconvenient' areas of 'factory'-type employment that requires more shift work. Similarly, new technology has led to de-skilling of clerical and secretarial work and there has been a growth of 'flexible' working arrangements, including a large increase in part-time work that continues to associate a low value exclusively to women.

Similar trends are in evidence in other EC countries which are quickly responding to the growing competition in the Europeanisation and internationalisation of the banking world. Within Europe the liberalisation of the movement of finance means that it will be possible to locate a branch of a bank in another EC country. This may have a particularly important impact on women in some of the less developed regions of the EC, for instance in Spain or Portugal, where women are under-represented in banking in contrast to their northern European neighbours. This could lead to a much more significant feminisation of banking in these countries.

Social dumping

As competition grows in Europe different levels of wages, social security and social protection could leave some member states in a competitively weaker position than others. This is known as 'social dumping' and is defined as:

> the use of low levels of working conditions and social standards – below that which the productivity of the economy would normally justify – to improve market shares and competitiveness. (Commission of the EC, 1989a)

As a result of the factors affecting the competitive capacity of sectors and regions there are real fears expressed by some of the more prosperous European countries that their higher social standards, better pay and employment conditions could result in 'social dumping'. This could involve the substitution of capital for lower-skilled workers and a shift in production to the southern European countries whose lower wages appear competitively advantageous. Overall, it does raise the possibility of labour costs being reduced, of health and safety at work being eroded or neglected and working conditions becoming worsened. Despite being competitive regarding wages and social protection, southern European countries have poorer communications and could be left on the periphery of the core areas of development in the EC.

'Social dumping' is not new or unique to the EC. Indeed, employers have historically utilised women as a cheap source of labour precisely for these reasons. Nevertheless, the opening up of the internal market does increase the possibility of 'social dumping' becoming a reason for retaining jobs with low labour costs in order to remain competitive.

Alternatively it could lead to some of the more prosperous member states reducing their own labour costs to prevent 'social dumping' taking place. Some of the northern European countries with higher social security benefits and social protection are concerned about the effects that 'social dumping' could have on them, by suggesting the lowering of their more privileged and generous benefits to avoid a competitive disadvantage. Indeed, many of the campaigns, including those of the women's movement in Denmark against Danish entry into the EC in the early 1970s were based on the fear that the relatively high standards in Denmark would be forced down to the lower levels in other EC countries. In arguing for protection against 'social dumping', other European countries have looked towards the single market as an opportunity to raise their own social policies to the higher levels enjoyed in France, Denmark and Germany. Women in the UK have particularly welcomed the single market for this reason and have argued that the potential to improve access to social benefits, childcare and other social policies would markedly improve their relatively weak social position.

The aim underlying the Social Charter, passed in 1989, was to provide minimum levels of social protection at the EC level, in order to prevent social dumping taking place. The Social Charter is discussed further in Chapter 7.

Women's earnings

Women's earnings will also be affected by the operation of the internal market. 'Social dumping' could have a disastrous effect on women's earnings, particularly because many women work in industries where there are relatively low labour costs. The previous chapter showed how women's earnings have always lagged behind men's. This is despite the fact that all member states of the EC have passed equal pay laws and have adopted the 1975 directive on equal pay. There is no evidence to suggest that women's earnings will be enhanced through the single market. At one level fiercer competition could lead to the gap in unequal pay between men and women widening or becoming more depressed. However, at another there is a great potential for women's earnings to increase significantly in the higher-skilled occupations.

A wider understanding of women's access to income encompasses much more than their earnings. The Van Hemeldonck Report made it clear that earnings from paid employment were only one aspect of women's income, which also included income from social security benefits and allowances and the invisible earnings from belonging to a family, local or cooperative enterprise. Large numbers of women work in these 'grey areas', and while employed to help out with a family or small enterprise are not recorded in the statistics. Likewise, according to the report, more women than men are involved in 'moonlighting' and this provides the only source of income for large numbers of women.

Women in the peripheral regions of the EC

Unpaid family help or invisible work is more evident in the peripheral regions of the EC and in rural areas and in small enterprises. It involves work for no pay or social security benefits, but is nonetheless recorded in overall output of a family enterprise, for example a farm. The under-estimation and invisibility of women's contributions to the economic stability of small enterprises have consequences for the internal market. According to Van Hemeldonck:

> The local, or regional network could be upset if there were a temporary or permanent exodus of the more highly-skilled and flexible members of the local community (men) in the wake of a deterioration in th profitability of the small enterprise. (European Parliament, 1988, p. 6)

The advent of the single market, growing competition and the squeezing out of small enterprises makes this situation all the more likely. If this arises, it would be the women left in these peripheral and rural areas who would continue to provide domestic and caring roles and their traditional jobs in addition to the male jobs. Van Hemeldonck concludes that:

> If the EEC fails to produce legislation recognizing the economic importance and the occupational hazards faced by women in agriculture, particularly in the peripheral regions, and assuming that the existing social structure in those regions remains unchanged, the position of women will get worse because it is mainly the men who will be mobile and the women will have to cope on their own with worsening working conditions. (European Parliament, 1988, p. 6)

In some senses women living in the peripheral regions of the EC could benefit from the opening up of the internal market. Better communications, transport and programmes to improve regional infrastructure could make it easier and cheaper to move people and goods from one region to another, from the periphery to the centre and vice versa. Van Hemeldonck argues that:

> The living conditions of women in remote regions will improve as a result. Hospitals, schools, information centres and shopping centres

will become more accessible. Telecommunications will become cheaper and more widespread, and hence it will be possible to set up for women, even in remote areas, information and closed-circuit education and training programmes. (European Parliament, 1988, p. 6)

At best this is a very optimistic view of the gains to be made for the regions, and may be insufficient to counter depopulation, unemployment and underemployment in the poorer regions of the EC. Improved communications and transport could directly disadvantage the traditional patterns of production that women are involved in. Enhanced access to the regions will bring more mass produced goods onto local markets in direct competition with locally produced goods and services. This could have a devastating effect on women's employment in local and regional craft and farming enterprises. EC assistance and funding for local employment initiatives will, therefore, be of crucial importance in the single market.

FREE MOVEMENT OF LABOUR

Women and mobility

Free movement of labour is fundamental to the internal market. EC nationals and their families have the right to residence in EC countries. However, it is important to distinguish between migration and mobility when discussing free movement of labour. Migration has come to mean the movement of the unqualified and unskilled, while mobility has become that of the qualified and skilled. The question of migration is looked at below.

Experience in Europe has shown that men have been more mobile and less constrained by family and local ties than women. The Single European Market encourages much greater mobility of labour and there is no doubt that free movement of labour will enable women and men to move about the Community in search of better training and job advancement. Most evident is that women and men living in the poorer and more peripheral regions of the community will have access to these benefits. With higher concentration of employment and skilled labour in core areas of the EC, it is likely that some regions in the EC will experience even greater levels of depopulation than hitherto.

Experience has also shown, moreover, that skilled and trained workers are more likely to be mobile than unskilled or semi-skilled manual workers. For this reason alone, women will have poorer access to mobility than men, because of their lower levels of training and their concentration in unskilled or semi-skilled occupations.

Population decline in Ireland, for instance, has continued over centuries for this very reason, although historically it has been unskilled manual workers who have migrated to the UK. In more recent years it has been young Irish people, often with training, skills and university education, who have left their country of origin in search of better job opportunities abroad. Indeed more young Irish women have taken up these opportunities than ever before. Ireland is one EC country where demographic changes will lead to a larger indigenous population. Unless employment growth matches population growth, further depopulation could result.

Because men in all EC countries have better access to education and training, particularly in the areas of demand for skilled labour, and because men are more mobile, it will be women who are left behind to live and work in areas of rural and urban decline. Even where a partner is temporarily mobile and absent from the family, there is a strong likelihood that family ties will be reduced, responsibilities for payment of maintenance or alimony neglected, and the full responsibility for childcare resting with women. This could further disadvantage women's access to employment and could result in lower living standards for women. In cases where a divorced partner moves to another country, there are problems in the differing coverage and protection given to court rulings in EC countries relating, for instance, to maintenance payments. The lack of harmonisation of marital and family law within the EC leads to further inconsistencies and uncertainties for many women.

Social security benefits and allowances are of crucial importance in facilitating free movement. The harmonisation of social security throughout the EC is particularly vital for women moving from one country to another. Wide variations in social security provisions means that it is hard for women to make choices about moving to another country to work. A woman working in France may not be able to claim her rights to the good levels of maternity provision or childcare if she chose to work in the UK. There are also wide variations in the extent to which women are treated as dependants, based on their husband's status, as opposed to having independent entitlements to social security, as is the case in Denmark.

Social security arrangements are vitally important to women. They include child benefits, maternity benefits, supplements for looking after a child in the home and caring for the sick, disabled or the elderly. The existence of these benefits in one country may affect a woman's choice to take advantage of free movement of labour. Conversely, since women's patterns of mobility tend to be traditionally determined by their husband's patterns, the provision of harmonised benefits in all EC countries will be important to ensure that women do not lose out in moving from one country to another. Without harmonisation women's mobility will be further restricted.

Women and migration

In 1987 it was estimated that between 8 and 15 million non-EC nationals live in the EC, of whom 40–60 per cent are women. Migrant workers include immigrants, second and third generations of non-EC citizens, migrant workers, refugees and asylum seekers. They are the 'thirteenth state' in Europe, holding different rights to EC citizens. It is important to distinguish between EC citizens and residents. For most migrant workers in the EC their access to full legal, civil and political rights is dependent on citizen status.

Migrant women from both within and outside the EC are often extremely disadvantaged. Their incomes, working conditions and social situations are markedly inferior to those of EC nationals. A much higher proportion of migrant women work than women who are EC nationals. Many migrated as dependants rather than as workers, and are overwhelmingly represented in low-paid, insecure and vulnerable forms of employment. According to Pauline Conroy-Jackson:

> This position of dependency is not so much a source of discrimination as a question of legal vulnerability, limiting migrant women to illegal and unprotected work as domestic workers, industrial cleaners or homeworkers, without residence or work permits. (Commission of the EC, 1990b, p. 59)

Black and ethnic minority women are particularly concentrated in the vulnerable and sensitive industries, are more likely to be involved in atypical work, and are the least mobile group in the community. They are also less likely to have opportunities for good training, essential for access to the new job opportunities opening up with the single market.

Many migrant women in the EC have neither residence nor work permits. They are commonly defined as a 'problem' rather than as a resource, and there is little recognition of the important economic contribution many of them make to European economies. The experience of racial divisions and of insitutional racism in Europe leaves many black and ethnic minority people in weak positions. They do not have access to the same levels of power, privilege and status enjoyed by white people. Moreover, black women's experiences of racism are compounded by their gender. Black women enter the stage of 1992 on an unequal footing. Their lower levels of job status, pay and conditions of employment, combined with experiences of racism, mean that they are likely to be the losers rather than the winners in the single market. According to Jane Goldsmith (1990):

> If black and ethnic minority communities have been further marginalised by the European Community, black and ethnic minority women have been even more so. They continue to remain invisible in statistics, research planning, and decision making. Their strengths, value and contribution to the economies of Europe in paid and unpaid work remains unquantified and unrecognised. They do not feature in the male economists' visions of Europe. (p. 4)

The rise in racism and xenophobia in all EC countries has received growing attention at the EC level. A report by Glyn Ford (MEP) on behalf of the European Parliament's Committee of Inquiry into Racism and Xenophobia, in October 1990, confirmed this trend (European Parliament, 1990b). The Committee called for a new charter to protect and enhance the rights of migrant workers.

The vision of a new Europe has to be seen within the context of cultural identity and a European history of colonisation. Speaking at the intergovernmental conference in Bruges in 1988 Margaret Thatcher was clear that: 'From our perspective today, surely what strikes us most is our common experience. For instance, the story of how Europeans explored and colonised and – yes, without apology – civilised much of the world is an extraordinary tale of talent, skill and courage.'

The socio-legal position of black and ethnic minority people living in the UK differs from that of other ethnic minority groups in Europe, many of whom, like the black British population, sought work in the more prosperous colonial countries of Western Europe. For most 'migrant' workers in other EC states their position is seen as temporary (though rarely such). They are denied full political and civil rights, and are rarely protected in law from direct or indirect racism (Runneymead Trust, 1987).

Migrant and refugee groups in Europe are concerned that the single market is leading to a 'fortress' Europe. The opening up of barriers to not only trade and capital, but also people, means that if free movement of labour is to become a reality for EC citizens, then it is argued that the external barriers to the movement of non-EC citizens and goods have to be strengthened. As a result the run-up to the completion of the internal market led to a whole series of debates about tightening immigration controls, reinforcing Eurocentric traditions, and linking discussions to combat illegal immigration to those to combat terrorism and drug trafficking (Gordon, 1989). In many senses we can witness a new politics of a Europe of exclusion rather than inclusion. This will result in more immigration controls and greater restrictions on the movement of third country nationals, that will further disadvantage the position of migrant workers and refugees in Europe.

Black and ethnic minority people in the UK, in contrast to many 'migrant' workers in EC countries, do have civil and political rights, albeit constrained by restrictive nationality and immigration legislation. Given that the politics of a Europe of exclusion is tied up with the control of illegal immigration and that this in turn is tied up with 'race', this inevitably has an effect on the way that black and ethnic minority people are viewed in the context of free movement of labour within the EC. The access of black people, who are full EC citizens, to free movement may be restricted by racist views that black = migrant = illegal. To discuss the issue of 'race' in the EC inevitably leads to a discussion of illegal immigration or the 'migrant problem'. There is a danger that the removal of internal border controls could lead to greater controls within EC countries. These could lead to nationality checks, through the production of a passport in hospitals, in the receipt of housing or other welfare benefits and on the streets. This in turn could lead to greater racial harrassment and discrimination for black and ethnic minority EC nationals. External immigration into the EC will also become more restricted and it is widely believed that an EC immigration policy would be one of the most restrictive of the member states' practices in the EC, at the 'lowest common denominator'.

Large numbers of black people who are legally resident and have full citizenship rights in the UK will be denied free movement of labour. These are the people who have chosen to retain their passports of their country of origin, something not accounted for in EC rules on free movement of labour. This particularly affects black and ethnic minority women who are less likely to have taken naturalisation than their husbands or fathers. Moreover the lack of recognition of third-country qualifications further restricts the intra-community movement, at a time when the EC is developing standardisation and harmonisation of diplomas, degrees and professional qualifications.

4 Making the EC Work for Women

INTRODUCTION

This chapter looks at how the EC represents women's interests and the extent to which women have access to and are able to influence and affect the policy-making process. It will start by looking at how women have influenced the institutional structure of the EC and the ways in which women are attempting to make the EC work for them. It will finish with a discussion of the different legislative frameworks that have been used to develop policies for women.

Women have successfully influenced national government policies, and more recently EC policy, to secure improvements in their legal status. This has resulted in numerous campaigns and actions to challenge inequality and male dominance at both the national and international level. Some of these campaigns have focused on changing established approaches to policy-making and in securing legislative change. There is no doubt that the women's movement has been vital in getting issues onto the policy agenda, in identifying problems and educating the public, the media, political elites and policy makers on the need for legislative change. According to Vicky Randall (1987):

> The present wave of feminism has undoubtedly had an impact on policy; it has brought to the fore and redefined issues previously neglected, helped to secure major changes in official policy and ensured that these are at least partially implemented. (p. 262)

The contemporary women's movement is difficult to define, not least because of its wide-ranging theoretical, ideological and organisational bases. In a very broad sense these range from more traditional rights organisations (such as the Townswomen's Guild), women's sections working within political parties and interest groups, to more autonomously organised feminist groups working around specific issues, often in an *ad hoc* way. The latter have been influenced by feminist theory that criticised patriarchy for its subordination of women in all areas of life. The way in which women's interests

63

influence policy varies. According to Joni Lovenduski (1988), these range from separatist to integrationist strategies, *ad hoc* movements and direct action, as well as the use of more direct lobbying and pressure group tactics which 'seek either individually or collectively to defend and expand women's economic, political and social cultural rights' (p. 113). There has been growing support for women's demands and the promotion and representation of women's interests has been extensive and influential.

This is not surprising given the growing role of both the national and European state. It has brought with it new forms of patriarchal control as a result of a shift from private patriarchy (within the family and the home) to new forms of state patriarchy. Despite this the concept of 'state feminism' has been used to describe the role of state intervention in national and EC policy to promote women's pay and employment opportunities. Ruth Neilson (1981) argues that 'national law is . . . considerably more marked by patriarchal traits than Community law. The EC can hardly be said to have entered into an alliance with partriarchy'.

The EC, in contrast to many national governments, has been fairly open to pressure from women. Of particular importance to many women is that EC policy has had and continues to have a large impact on national policy-making.

There is considerable evidence to suggest that women and women's interests are not represented in corporatist policy-making channels, in trade unions, employers' associations or governing elites (Randall, 1987, Lovenduski, 1986, Mayo, 1977). However, in the 1980s and 1990s women became more influential in these formal channels of representation, particularly in trade unions. In contrast women are much more visible in *ad hoc* political campaigns and pressure groups, in consumer and promotional groups. Although important in pressuring for change, these are less likely to be taken seriously than the more powerful corporate interests.

Nevertheless, women have had a growing influence on the EC in a number of different ways. This has involved the development of women's networks across Europe, the growing use of feminist research in the development of policy in the Commission, the support of the European Parliament Women's Committee for women's demands throughout the EC, the growth of the European women's movement and the growing participation of women's organisations and voluntary groups in lobbying. These influences are increasingly being felt in the more established and formal decision-making bodies in Europe. They have been effected through the Women's Committees of the European Parliament and the European Trade Union Confederation (ETUC), and within the various sections in the EC Commission dealing with women's issues.

It is clear that the representation and promotion of women's interests has amounted to a growing influence in policy-making at the EC level and this has led to a much wider focus for policies to include all aspects of women's lives. There has also been a growing interest amongst feminists in developing cross-national links in the recognition, first, of the gains to be made from EC membership, and second, to ensure that the single market does not lead to women being disadvantaged by the new forms of competition in Europe. The role of these groups and of the initiatives developed now adds up to a sizeable influence on EC policy. However, they face an enormous challenge in the single market, where producer interests are dominating this increasingly competitive area.

PRESSURE FROM WOMEN

The development of an EC policy for women did not, in the early days of the EC, lead to a movement of women pushing for extensions to policies and influencing the policy-making process. However, there has been a growth of this interest both within the EC institutions and from women throughout the EC. The EC has developed policies that are closely connected with the labour market. These policies have to be rooted in the Treaty of Rome where there is no reference to the non-working population and to women's roles outside paid work. Policies have also been closely linked with the somewhat abstract notion of equality that many feminists have rejected. As a result some feminists have found the EC to be of little relevance to their lives. However, the widening of the debate about women's lives, in particular in the European Parliament, has been a response to the need to broaden this limited policy framework.

Within the EC institutions themselves there has been a growing awareness of the disadvantages women face in society. Different EC institutions hold varying levels of power and influence and pressure from women within the institutions has been felt in a number of different ways. (Appendix 1 gives a detailed discussion of the different institutions of the EC, their powers, roles and functions. Appendix 2 shows how women can influence the EC process.)

Much of the influence from women has been a direct result of pressure from women within the Commission and the European Parliament seeking to redress the high profile given to men's interests in policy-making, in particular in the Council of Ministers. It has led to the development of new policy instruments and a subtle and often painstaking process of educating male political elites to recognise women's specific needs.

The role of the EC Commission in promoting women's rights

In this respect information has been an important tool for the Commission. Its distance from women in the EC was confirmed in a survey carried out by the Commission where 62 per cent of respondents did not know what the Community was doing for women (Commission of the EC, 1975). In response to the lack of information and the distance of the EC from many women, two institutional mechanisms were created within the Commission in the 1970s. These were the Information Office of Women's Organisations and Press (in Directorate General X) and the Women's Bureau for questions concerning the Employment and Equal Treatment of Women, later renamed the Equal Opportunities Unit (Directorate General V). However, they have been under-staffed and under-resourced and have suffered from the general low priority given to women's issues in the EC budget, compared to, for instance, agriculture.

The Equal Opportunities Unit has grown in importance and although by 1990 it had a staff of 16 it remains under-staffed and under-resourced. Despite these limitations it has provided a vital source of information and networking for women in the EC and has played an increasingly important role in the development of new policies and in drawing up new legislation. However, the Equal Opportunities Unit has often been hampered by the reluctance of the Council of Ministers to take women's issues seriously, and has frequently been forced to compromise its policy proposals in this light. In particular the Unit has come to rely more and more on the lobbying of women outside the EC institutions to win its arguments with the Council of Ministers.

A Women's Information Bureau was also set up in the Commission in the 1970s to establish contact and information exchanges between women's groups and organisations throughout the EC. This resulted in the publication of the bimonthly journal *Women of Europe*, translated into all Community languages and distributed free of charge to women throughout all member states. During the early

1980s, it also organised several conferences and seminars in several member states, in order to involve women's organisations in EC policy-making and informing women of the role of the EC in this area. According to Fausta Deshormes (1972):

> The informational role devolving on the European Commission is obviously one that tends to strengthen favourable attitudes among the general public . . . and to stimulate awareness among the vast mass of the population whose knowledge of the subject is scant or non-existent, but at the same time it must tend to arouse a political sense.

The Commissioners and Commission officials often take strong political roles in promoting new policies and work closely with pressure groups to seek support for their policies. Indeed, the political machinery in Brussels is tightly bound up with interest and lobbying groups, many of whom use professional lobbying organisations or develop their own, with offices close to the Commission. As a result the Commission consults a whole range of different groups, including national officials, experts and representatives of interested groups, in drawing up policy. In this sense the Commission has become receptive to pressure group activity. This is reflected in the openness of its policy-making structure and its attempts to involve a wide range of participants in policy-making.

Consultations have correspondingly been established through the Commission's Equal Opportunities Unit. This has involved representatives from member states' official equal opportunities commissions and committees, but not those representing the interests of the vast range of autonomous groups that form the women's liberation movement in Europe. Consultations began in 1974 where representatives met with the Commission on an *ad hoc* basis and since 1980 in a permanent Advisory Committee. The Committee advises the Commission on policy measures and although meeting only twice a year, with limited financial resources, has been important in injecting fresh ideas and propelling the EC forward in a positive way. The group has been openly critical of the Council of Ministers' failure to take account of its proposals and has forced the Commission to widen and extend its policies. Catherine Hoskyns (1986) demonstrates how the meetings held in the *ad hoc* group surrounding the drafting of the equal treatment directive were 'qualitatively different' from those in the Council of Ministers' working group, 'the reason being that the women took the issue seriously (and had some knowledge of the situations being discussed) whereas by and large the men did not' (p. 216).

The Advisory Committee has been of immense importance in co-ordinating the views and common problems facing women in the member states. It continues to be an important source of pressure on the Commission and has directly forced the Commission to continue to reflect women's interests, especially when at times the Commission has been reluctant to extend its policies in this area.

Many of the established professional lobbying groups in Brussels have also set up their own women's sections and have put increasing pressure on the Commission to broaden policy goals for women and initiate new legislation. These include the Farmers' Lobby, the European Youth Forum, and the Confederation of Family Organisations in the European Community (COFACE). In addition, the European Trade Union Confederation (ETUC) Women's Committee has developed important links with the Commission for this purpose.

The Commission has shown an awareness of feminist issues and the need to involve women in discussions about EC policy. Indeed, it was at the forefront of initiating and giving some funding for the European Women's Lobby, which was formally launched in September 1990. It has also given small grants and assistance to women throughout the EC in the setting up of networks and exchanges, for instance, through the European Network of Women.

Networking has increasingly become a vital tool for the Commission in injecting fresh ideas and pressure for new women's policies and at the same time keeping the Commission on its toes. In 1982 a new mechanism for monitoring progress in member states and for suggesting new policy initiatives saw the creation of a number of networks of experts, with representatives from each member state, attached to the Equal Opportunities Unit. The networks of experts have been of considerable importance to the Equal Opportunities Unit and have enabled national monitoring to take place, which the Commission was ill-placed to conduct itself. This in turn has given an additional level for the Commission to develop new policies based on experts' reports and recommendations. There are networks covering childcare, the diversification of occupational choices, women in the labour market, the implementation of the equality directives, equal opportunities in education, the IRIS network on training schemes for women, women in local employment initiatives, higher and public service, women in industry and women in the media.

The Women's Committee of the European Parliament

At a political level women in the European Parliament have been a vital source of support for women in the EC. The first direct elections to the European Parliament in 1979 saw the highest proportion of women represented in the European Parliament (69 out of 410 elected members), a larger proportion than that returned to national parliaments. Seventeen per cent of members elected in 1984 were women, a similar proportion to that elected in 1979, compared to 10 per cent elected to national parliaments. Larger numbers of women in the European Parliament did not automatically guarantee a greater representation on women's issues. However, a great majority of these new women members actively campaigned, in the Parliament, for further policies for women, through questions to the Commission and through their representation on various committees.

The European Parliament first took up the issue of the status of women through the formation of an Ad Hoc Women's Committee in 1979. A resolution was passed that recognised the lack of attention paid to women in the general committees in the Parliament and was followed by the preparation of a major report and a full one-day debate on the position of women in the EC. The Ad Hoc Committee on Women's Rights aimed to create a lobby that would cut across both national and political boundaries within the Parliament. In interviews in 1984, several members of the Committee spoke openly about the enormous success of this approach, not least in achieving greater cooperation between different political groups. According to Ien Van den Houvel (Socialist Group) this had been achieved in a 'remarkable way and is something that we can be proud of, its very special this women's co-operation' (interview, Strasbourg, 1983). However, two women from the the European Democratic Group, British Conservatives Gloria Hooper and Dame Shelagh Roberts, were clear that they joined the Committee in order to keep a check on the group. They both felt that the Committee ghettoised women's problems and that its brief was too wide (interview, Strasbourg, 1984).

In 1984 the Women's Committee became a formal and permanent committee in the Parliament. As with other parliamentary committees it is made up of representatives from all political groups within the Parliament. Although political differences are inevitable it appears that the Women's Committee reaches consensus on a wider range of issues than other committees. Much of this rests on agreement about the common problems and disadvantages that all women face and for

Mdm Dury, MEP, was based on the 'solidarity of women and how women want to build a different society'. However, it is evident that the Committee is taken more seriously by women on the left than by women on the right. Nevertheless, many of the liberal and Christian Democrat MEPs are very radical in their thinking and will often support socialist women colleagues on women's issues before supporting their own parties. The two UK Conservative members of the Committee, however, were often absent from meetings and there was a general view that they had given up on raising objections to proposals within the Committee, which was heavily dominated by women on the left. This has, however, threatened the existence and credibility of the Committee and its foundation on cross-political group representations.

The 1988 elections to the European Parliament brought a new generation of women MEPs committed to strengthening women's rights in Europe. This coincided with the Women's Committee being taken more seriously by the Parliament. This was particularly the case for issues discussed in 1990, where the socialist president of the Parliament gave high priority to women's issues, in a way that previous presidents had not always done. In interviews with members of the Women's Committee in 1990 it was evident that they felt that women's issues were being taken more seriously. Although it was recognised that some MEPs found the Committee to be a 'pain in the neck' they quietly tolerated their existence. The Chair of the Women's Committee, Christine Crawley, viewed it as:

> a continual thorn in the flesh of the male establishment. I see it as a source of controversial subject material as well as a very necessary monitoring and gingering up of the Commission, because in the last few years . . . they have become complacent, I believe, in their role, in people's eyes, as being good on women's issues. (Interview, Strasbourg, 1990)

It was clear to many members of the Women's Committee that the scope for influence had gone beyond that of changing attitudes to one that integrates the concerns of women into mainstream EC policy. As a result it has developed into a systematic monitoring of all EC legislation to see how far women's interests are represented and where the women's agenda lies. This is a particularly important development, it avoids the marginalisation of women's issues within the Committee and gives women's concerns a much higher profile than if they emanated from the Women's Committee itself. This is also evident in the work of the other parliamentary committees that most members also sit on. Here women's issues have been raised with more conviction and force in this process of mainstreaming women's issues throughout the Parliament.

The Women's Committee has acted as an important pressure group within the Parliament. The new role given to the Parliament in the Single European Act could, however, lead to problems for the Committee. It has in the past been less preoccupied with the scrutiny of legislation than in the writing of reports and proposals for new areas for action. The procedures on consultation and the system of having two readings in the Parliament means that more legislation is coming from the Council of Ministers. This often gives only a short time for the examination and scrutiny of proposals in the various committees and for amendment and debate in the plenary session. This places additional pressure on the time available for debating new non-legislative issues in the plenary session and has forced the Women's Committee to adopt its own recommendations in committee rather in Parliament. While this may be helpful in getting issues passed, it reduces the public and media profile given to issues discussed in plenary sessions and has less impact in changing attitudes.

Equally important have been attempts in the Parliament to upstage the Commission where it has been reluctant to issue a directive on a key issue of concern to women. Several attempts are being made in the Parliament to issue their own draft directives to the Commission. For instance, a draft directive on atypical work was presented to the Commission by Heinke Salish (German Socialist) and this was seen as a very important move in forcing the Commission to initiate and adopt their own directive. In 1990 the Women's Committee was considering issuing a similar draft directive on childcare in order to prompt the Commission into action, on an issue which the Parliament felt the Commission had neglected.

At both the EC and national level there has been a growing interest, amongst women's organisations and feminist groups from outside the institutions of the EC, in the impact that EC policies can have on women. For instance, the Rights of Women Europe Group (1983) published a book designed to mobilise feminist action and inform women of the substantial gains that can be made from the EC for women. Pressure directed to the EC was seen to be important at a time when the UK Government was not making any attempts to improve the position of women.

Centre for Research on European Women (CREW) and the European Network of Women (ENOW)

Outside the formal consultation process, an important European feminist network has developed. This was initiated by the Brussels-based Centre for Research on European Women (CREW), which has sought to monitor and review the progress of EC legislation through its regular CREW reports. In addition it provides research and consultancy to member states, women's organisations and the EC Commission. It has also provided women's groups throughout the EC with regular and updated information on the work of the EC institutions as well as running the Commission's immensely successful IRIS network on women's training.

This work led to the setting up of the European Network of Women (ENOW). This was a response to the growing interest amongst feminist groups in engaging in EC-level discussions and in developing an EC-wide lobby. It has been designed to bring greater pressure on the EC institutions, to continue with and extend their policy for women and to monitor the implementation of policy at the national level. ENOW began its work by developing a lobby in Brussels, and this led to the establishment of a network of women throughout Europe for the purpose of running EC-wide campaigns.

Meetings were organised in towns and cities throughout the EC in 1983, and in 1984 the first ENOW conference was held in Brussels, with some sponsorship from the Commission. The network has emphasised the growing need to look at the position of women with a European focus and to seek common solutions to common problems. However, its work has been hampered by a lack of resources to develop a strong lobby, in contrast to some of the more established and incorporated interest groups at the EC level. Indeed, the network has survived because of the commitment of women at a grass-roots level who have worked voluntarily with limited resources. Its organisation has been based on feminist principles and it has remained committed to staying in touch with women at the grass-roots level. Its existence has had strong support amongst women both in the Commission and the European Parliament. In 1988 ENOW organised the first of a series of seminars on women in poverty in

Europe and has developed the first European women's network on poverty.

The European Women's Lobby

The setting up of the European Women's Lobby takes these influences a stage further. The EC Commission saw the merits of such a Europe-wide lobby in response to the importance of lobbying to the Brussels machinery and the general under-representation of women's interests within it. As a result it initiated a lobby with the aim of drawing women from all member states into lobbying for change. This has been an important development and a recognition that is attached to the importance of wide-scale support for women, to ensure that gains are not lost and that progress is made. The European Women's Lobby was first proposed in 1980 and had the backing of established women's organisations throughout Europe. In 1987 at the 4th European Colloquy of Women's Associations of the 12 member states of the EC, the European Women's Lobby was established.

Its aim is to ensure that there is continual progress in policy development and that a constant dialogue is maintained between women's organisations and the Community institutions. It is primarily seen as a pressure group. A permanent office is to be located in Brussels alongside other already established lobbies. At the end of the first meeting, in 1987, several resolutions were passed, including the call for faster progress towards equal opportunities in a united Europe and the creation of an influential pressure group of women's interests at the EC level. The first meetings of the European Women's Lobby were held in the UK in October and November 1988, in Glasgow, Belfast, Cardiff and London. These were organised by the UK offices of the European Commission. The Lobby was officially launched in Brussels in September 1990 when the first General Assembly was held. The Assembly was made up of more than 70 delegates of national and European voluntary women's organisations, from which a bureau and a secretary-general were elected. The role of the Lobby and its priorities are further discussed in Chapter 8.

European Trade Union Confederation (ETUC) Women's Committee

The ETUC Women's Committee exists to coordinate the work of women in trade unions across the EC. Its membership extends beyond

EC countries to cover trade unions from the European Free Trade Association countries. However, it has developed strong links with the institutions of the EC and has formal representations on a variety of committees. The Committee meets twice a year and has one representative from each union centre with three representatives from the UK TUC, the Irish ITUC and the German DGB. According to Beatrice Hertogs (of the secretariat of the Women's Committee) the Women's Committee is 'the only body that gives women the opportunity to express and form collective opinions . . . you can see what you have in common, to establish what is feasible at the European level' (interview, Brussels, 1990).

The forming of collective opinions and strategies is seen to be vital for women across Europe to enable them to work within a European perspective and engage in Europe-wide lobbying. The Women's Committee does not directly lobby the EC Commission; this is carried out by a formal link with the secretariat of the ETUC. It does, however, have a wide range of formal and informal links with a variety of other women's lobbying bodies. It is represented on the European Women's Lobby, although the Women's Committee views that lobbying through the ETUC is strategically better for women in trade unions. The Advisory Committee on Equal Opportunities in the Commission, which has five observers from the ETUC, is increasingly taking the role of the ETUC Women's Committee seriously. The Advisory Group is seen as one of the most active bodies working for women in the EC. However, the role of the Women's Committee is restricted by a lack of resources. It faces greater problems than other ETUC committees in bringing women together at a European level, adding an additional burden to women's lack of time to combine union work with domestic and childcare responsibilities. The priorities and role of the ETUC Women's Committee are discussed further in Chapter 8.

Equal opportunities committees and commissions

In all EC countries statutory bodies exist to advise national governments on issues relating to women. The levels of power and influence depend on their relationship to statutory bodies, their levels of funding and the legal importance attached to them. It is only in the UK, Ireland and Denmark that quasi independent bodies have been set up, whereas in other EC countries these are bodies attached to national ministries. They are represented on the Commission's Advisory Group on Women. Many of these bodies are finding their roles in Europe to be too tightly controlled by the Commission's own priorities and restrictions. As a result there is a growing feeling that these bodies should also meet independently of the Commission and develop their own strategies for women necessitated by closer European links in the single market.

EUROPEAN COMMUNITY LEGISLATION

European Community legislation takes a number of forms, where a distinction is made between primary and secondary legislation. Primary legislation is set out in the Treaty of Rome. Treaty provisions override national law and are directly applicable in member states. However, the supremacy of European Community law is not always directly applicable in the first instance, and it has often taken cases in the European Court of Justice (for instance, under Article 119 on equal pay) to establish this principle.[1] The Treaty of Rome also makes it possible for new legislative provisions, secondary legislation, to be made.[2] These include regulations, directives, decisions, opinions, recommendations, and resolutions. They vary in their enforcement and legal weight and the extent to which national implementing measures need to be introduced and include:

- regulations which introduce new law that overrides national law;
- directives, which are binding, but require member states to implement national provisions to achieve the objectives of the directive (they include directives on equal pay, equal treatment, equality in state social security schemes, equality in occupational social security schemes, equal treatment for the self-employed). A number of draft directives covering the areas of part-time work, temporary work, parental leave, equal retirement age and the reversal of the burden of proof in equality cases have been rejected;
- decisions which are addressed to either an individual or member state, which again are binding, but which have to be implemented into national legislation;
- opinions, recommendations and resolutions which are non-binding statements of policy (a significant number of opinions, recommendations and resolutions have been passed, including three equality action programmes, dignity at work, women and unemployment, positive action and reorganisation of working time).

Appendix 3 lists all of the legal initiatives affecting women that have been either proposed or passed since the EC was formed in 1957.

Deciding on the type of legislation to be used is closely tied up with the prevailing political objectives in the EC. It is also related to the type of policy that is being proposed. The introduction of directives affecting women's pay and employment in the 1970s took place in a political environment that was receptive to a widening of policy in this area. However, the political environment in the 1980s led to a greater use of the legally weaker opinions, recommendations and resolutions as legislative actions. This approach has been a solution to the considerable pressure that has been building up for the passing of more controversial policies that are wider in scope than the policies proposed in the 1970s. It has also been a response by some member states, particularly the UK, which have been keen to restrict the development of policy for women.

The development of EC policy has taken a distinctly incremental path. Nevertheless, the legal provisions of the Treaty of Rome have often been interpreted in an imaginative way. Although EC policy-making has been characterised by piecemeal and slow progress, and sometimes inertia, it has enabled legislation to develop in response to changing social and economic priorities. It has also increasingly led to pressure from both within and outside the EC institutions to take greater account of the role of women in European integration.

The Treaty of Rome gives important and, as such, constitutional guidelines about the nature of policy. It therefore plays an important role in determining the nature and scope of subsequent policy developments. Of equal importance to EC policy making is that there is a wide diversity of policy processes within the EC.

It is useful to consider this in the context of a policy network where policy-making takes place in several tiers. Here policy is formulated both within the EC institutions and within national governments, administrations and interest groups. In this sense policy-making at the EC level is not markedly different from policy making at the national level and while the former can be seen to be an extension of the latter's policy-making, it is important to see the two roles as linked. Any policy that has a direct impact on a member state will necessarily involve important relationships with national policy-makers and interest groups. As a result there is a large network of organisations and groups (both governmental and non-governmental) who participate in the EC decision-making process.

It is certainly the case that in the area of policies affecting women's pay and employment, negotiation takes place with national governments and interest groups. Moreover, it is clear that member states have retained their own sovereignty as the EC has developed:

> Member States continue to exist as self-confident nation states and to exercise their responsibilities accordingly. They try to regain the freedom of action which the Community has taken from them by seeking to influence Community policy. The result is that the position of the Member States in the Community institutions is certainly stronger now than intended in the Treaties. (Laffan, 1983)

The influence of the nation state has ensured that the EC remains sensitive to national wishes. Thus, while the Commission may be developing or wanting to develop wide-ranging policies, their role is often constrained by the intergovernmental nature of the EC in the Council of Ministers. Nevertheless, the EC's policies affecting women have been successful in setting new standards of practice that are far higher than those of any member state. There is no doubt that a growing and effective lobby of women's interests has contributed to this. The next chapter will go on to look at how this policy has developed since 1957.

Notes

1. In *Defrenne* v. *Sabena*, case 43/75 (1979) *European Court Report* 445.
2. Under Articles 100 and 235 of the Treaty of Rome.

5 Developing Policies for Women in the EC, 1957–86

INTRODUCTION

The setting up of the European Community in 1957 spearheaded a series of policies affecting the rights of women in paid employment. These policies have had the effect of coordinating national legislation and standardising policy throughout the EC. At times this has been at a higher level than exists in any member state, which has been forced, often against its will, to monitor its own legislation and where necessary to introduce reforms that bring it in line with EC law.

EC policies for women have developed in four distinct stages. Each stage has been characterised by differing economic, political and social policy-making objectives. This chapter looks at the first three stages, up to 1986. Chapter 7 goes on to look at how EC policy for women has had an impact on women in the UK and the fourth stage of development, beyond 1986, is discussed in Chapter 8 in the light of policy developments in the Single European Market.

The first stage (1957–69) set the legal framework that enabled further policies to be developed after 1969. It saw the inclusion of Article 119 in the Treaty of Rome calling for equal pay for equal work. However, little was done to improve the position of women in the labour market until the 1970s. The second stage (1969–78) was an important and positive era in the development of EC policy for women. It saw the introduction of new directives and a much greater awareness of the disadvantages women face at work. The third stage (1978–86) was more concerned with consolidating the gains of the 1970s at a time of growing unemployment and economic decline. Gradually women became much more vocal in pressurising the EC for change both within the institutions of the EC and outside. This began to be felt in the 1970s and became more forceful in the 1980s as the women's movement began articulating its demands.

FIRST STAGE: ECONOMIC DEVELOPMENT, 1957-69

This stage saw the original six members of the EC developing the legal framework for the operation of a common market, which began with the signing of the Treaty of Rome in 1957. Social measures were seen as subordinate to the overriding economic priorities of setting up an economic community. It was strongly motivated by political and economic goals, rather than by the direct pursuit of social goals. The inclusion of Article 119 in the Treaty of Rome, calling for equal pay for equal work, followed the economic priorities of setting up an economic common market. Women were not organised at the EC level nor was there any recognition of either women's interests or the disadvantages women face in the labour market in the formal policy-making structure.

From the Treaty it is possible to identify four main areas of thinking on what can be loosely called the Treaty's social philosophy:

1. The principle of free movement of labour within the EC necessitated policies to ensure equal treatment for EC migrant workers and their families.
2. It was thought that the competitive position of member states should not be affected by their social responsibilities if they were found to be more numerous or more advanced in some states than others.
3. In order to improve understanding about working conditions, collaboration between member states was encouraged.
4. At a time of rapid economic change, training programmes were necessary to enhance occupational and geographic mobility in the EC. This led to the setting up of the European Social Fund.

The original six member states had created or were in the process of creating their own national welfare systems, and indeed, saw themselves as being capable of doing so in the future. However, at this stage no one knew what effect a common market would have on wage levels, employment and the standard of living. Of particular importance was that the Treaty left scope for future action if this was found to be necessary. This placed the Commission in a strong position to develop and initiate new social policies designed to benefit women directly. The setting up of a common market also contained a broad socioeconomic goal. This was that economic expansion, brought about by the freeing of tariff barriers to trade and free movement of labour, goods and services would enhance and accelerate standards of living. It was unclear how far integration would benefit some groups of workers, for example women, whose economic position could not be improved solely through economic expansion. In this respect the limited definition of social policy was gender-neutral. Patriarchal policy-making was clearly evident, as the objectives of securing a common market failed to recognise sexual divisions in the labour market and the disadvantaged position of women in society. It was only by default that women received some attention, in relation to equal pay, in the Treaty of Rome.

The question of social costs

The ambivalence to social policy and the consequent failure to develop policies for women can be charted within the context of a number of important policy documents (Robbins, 1952; Ohlin, 1956; Spaak, 1965). For those thinking of European integration in the 1950s, ideas were dominated by a number of agreed objectives. At the forefront was the immediate need to reconstruct the damaged economies of war-devastated Western Europe, much of which was under the guidance and instruction of the American-led Marshall Plan. Social policy was seen as an ideologically less important and pressing front for action than economic production, the liberalisation of trade and the opening up of trade barriers. As a result it was seen that improved living and working conditions would result from increased productivity: 'the most important contribution of freer trade to the raising of living standards is through its effects on economic growth' (Ohlin Report, 1956, para. 25).

As far as social action was concerned, this was only seen as necessary where free trade caused side effects for some groups of people and some industries. The overriding emphasis rested on the assumption that social action was only important where social charges impeded competition between states where it was believed that 'competition from countries with lower labour standards *may* be unfair' (Ohlin Report, 1956, para. 80).

Equal pay for men and women was seen within this context, on economic rather than social grounds. It was not intended to be of benefit to women, but rather to the competitive capacity of member states. Countries applying the principle of equal pay would be put in an unfair position compared to those countries paying lower wages to women, especially in female-dominated occupations and industries. France was particularly concerned about social costs, having already introduced equal pay. Arguing on behalf of employers, the French government felt social charges paid in France were higher than in other countries. This they stated would lead to an artificial competitive disadvantage, especially in the textile industry which employed large numbers of women. Despite disagreement amongst the governments of prospective member states about the need for harmonising social charges, France refused to sign the Treaty of Rome unless equal pay was included.

The result was a rather awkward concession to France, there being no mention in the Treaty of Rome of competition, and the only reason given for harmonisation being the need to promote improved working conditions and an improved standard of living. No effective means of implementation was attached to Article 119, and as a result member states saw no real necessity to commit themselves to developing new legal measures on equal pay. By accident rather than by design the signatories to the Treaty of Rome had laid the foundations for the development of EC policy for women, by the inclusion of Article 119 calling for equal pay for equal work.

Article 119

Article 119, calling for equal pay for equal work, has a direct bearing on the principle of equality since it overrides national law. It provides that:

Each Member State shall during the first stage ensure and subsequently maintain the application of the principle that men and women should receive equal pay for equal work.

For the purposes of this Article 'pay' means the ordinary basic minimum wage or salary and any other consideration whether in cash or in kind, which the worker receives, directly or indirectly, in respect of his employment from his employer.

Equal pay without discrimination based on sex means:

(a) that pay for the same work at piece rates shall be calculated on the basis of the same unit of measurement;

(b) that pay for work at time rates shall be the same for the same job.

From 1957 member states of the EC were committed to the implementation of equal pay for equal work. Article 119 has a direct effect on member states since it overrides national law. In practice, it took some time and a European Court judgment to establish the direct applicability of Article 119.

However, the application of equal pay into national legislation was very slow. Narrow legal provisions had been introduced in only four member states and the disparity between male and female rates of pay remained wide. In 1961, the Parliament and Commission reported on a lack of action and indifference to the principle. In practice, the fears of competitive disadvantage to France became less immediate as member states embarked on European integration. Since Article 119 was not designed to improve women's pay, nor confront inequalities and sexual divisions in the labour market, the continued disparity between male and female rates of pay was not a great concern to member states.

However, the Treaty of Rome placed a direct legal obligation on member states and the EC Commission, as 'guardian of the Treaty of Rome', was bound to ensure member states took the principle seriously. A more realistic definition of equal pay was developed by the Commission in 1960, to outlaw criteria of sex in wage fixing, while matters such as age, seniority and family status were excluded from the terms of equal work (Commission of the EC, 1960). This did little to encourage member states to introduce equal pay. In 1961 a Council Resolution called on member states to implement equal pay, with any differentials between male and female rates of pay eliminated by 31 December 1964 (Commission of the EC, 1962). Looking back, Evelyn Sullerot (1975) saw that the full implementation of the principle by 1964 had been:

> naively optimistic, but it turned out to be useful in as much as it encouraged rapid application in at least [two] fields, namely: elimination of discrimination in respect of statutory minimum wages and the revision of collective agreements to eliminate different job classification for men and women. (p. 67)

Member states began, slowly, to introduce legislation. Some used Article 119 as the model for their own legislation, making direct reference to EC obligations in domestic law, an approach taken, for instance, in Belgium.

SECOND STAGE: SOCIAL DEVELOPMENT, 1969–78

After 1969 the path of European integration took a new political direction. The second stage built on the priorities set out at the Hague Summit of 1969, to 'enlarge, deepen and extend' the EC, and was consolidated by the Paris Summit of 1971 that in turn led to the passing of the 1974 Social Action Programme. The social consequences of the common market had shown that economic growth had not been experienced evenly in all regions and amongst all groups of workers and women were identified as one group who had not benefited.

This was the most important stage in the development of policy, where three new directives on equal pay, equal treatment and equality in social security were adopted. This was particularly important for the UK, Ireland and Denmark who on entering the EC were obliged to adhere to EC law.

Women's interests began to be recognised in formal policy-making, and organised women's representation began to take shape. The late 1960s and early 1970s saw the growth of the new women's movement throughout Western Europe. The movement's concerns were increasingly being taken seriously by political parties and governments throughout the EC. For the first time, despite trade union opposition, women's organisations were being consulted about EC policy. This was a response to the growing voice of women and the need to prevent the 'corporate statism' of EC policy-making. This change in thinking was being felt in the EC Commission, where Fausta Deshormes (1979) commented that:

> Then, from 1970 on, the picture changed completely: the development of the Women's Liberation Movement . . . shed a brilliant light on the problem which had long been causing women to question the more 'traditional' organisations . . . women gradually became aware of their collective strength, the possibility now open to them of playing a part in events, and finally, a part that would promote change rather than conservation. (p. 49)

The political will to develop social change was present. National governments were becoming more aware of the problems inherent in postwar social development through the rediscovery of poverty, unemployment and the disadvantages faced by particular groups. The Commission was also keen to tap political support from women

by developing policies that went beyond the scope of existing national
legislation.

As a result the heads of the newly enlarged EC declared at the Paris
Summit in 1972 that they 'attached as much importance to rigorous
action in the social field as to the achievement of Economic and
Monetary Union'. The EC was searching hard to alter its image in
order to develop a 'human face' relevant to all people in all regions of
the EC. In this spirit a Social Action Programme was passed by the
Council of Ministers on 21 January 1974. It covered employment,
vocational training, improved working conditions, worker participation, collective bargaining at the European level and consumer
protection. It stated that 'economic expansion is not an end in itself,
but should result in an improvement in the quality of life as well as the
standard of living'.

Pay inequalities, discrimination and the disadvantaged position of
women in the labour market were becoming increasingly visible in the
EC. Backed by the Parliament, the Commission used Article 119 as a
catalyst to develop further legislation through the Social Action
Programme. This was seen to be particularly important given that
several member states had failed to implement equal pay and as three
new countries, the UK, Ireland and Denmark, joined the EC
(Commission of the EC, 1970, 1974a, 1974b; Sullerot, 1979).

One key Commission official, Jacqueline Nonnon, played a significant role in pressing the Commission to develop more wide-ranging
policies. She recognised that the legal provisions on pay had been
poorly implemented and that further instruments to help women
reconcile family responsibilities with work were needed. In this light
the Social Action Programme stated that 'immediate priority could be
given to the problems of providing facilities to enable women to
reconcile family responsibilities with job aspirations'.

This was seen to be necessary to ensure that the 'human face'
advocated by the Social Action Programme was one that included
women. Nonnon was later to head the 'Bureau for Questions
Concerning Women's Employment' set up in the Commission in
1974. An *ad hoc* group was set up to advise the Commission on
drawing up new women's policies. The group became a permanent
advisory committee in 1980 and has continued to be an important
source of pressure in the development of EC policy. This growing
profile given to equality issues coincided with an important judgment
in the European Court of Justice in 1974, *Defrenne* v. *Sabena*, that

established the direct applicability of Article 119 in member states and clarified some of its aims.

Despite the optimism of the Social Action Programme many of the proposals never reached the statute book. The oil crisis and changed economic priorities in the EC led to a shift in policy in 1975. However, substantial work had already been carried out to ensure the success of the plans for the three new directives on equal pay, equal treatment and social security, planned for International Women's Year in 1975.

The Equal Pay Directive

A directive on equal pay was passed in 1975, following a stormy period of negotiation by national government representatives in the Council of Ministers (1974a, 1974b). The negotiations were based more on political and ideological views about European integration itself, rather than on a direct concern with women's unequal pay. Views ranged from conservatism on the part of the UK, German and Irish delegations, signs of timidity by the Belgian, Italian and Luxembourg delegations and a positive attitude by the Dutch delegation. The UK and Danish governments were staunch supporters of national interests and were reluctant to extend the competence of the EC in any direction. The UK had one objective and that was to ensure that the directive fitted into the newly introduced, but not implemented, Equal Pay Act 1970. Such an approach at the negotiating table is not unusual, and the UK government has long been of the opinion that it would not ratify or adopt any international or European agreements on equal pay until it had adopted national legislation that met with such provisions.

The problem for the UK hinged on the technical application of 'equal value'. Not surprisingly the same discussions on equal value had been held in the UK Parliament when the Equal Pay Bill was discussed, where Secretary of State Barbara Castle was clear that equal value was an unworkable concept. It is no irony that the text offered by the UK delegation as a 'compromise' was that laid down in the Equal Pay Act. The final text of the directive accepted part of this compromise by making particular reference to the use of job evaluation schemes. In being a signatory of the directive, the UK was unequivocal in stating that the directive also implied that 'the circumstances in which work is concerned to have had an equal value attributed to it are where the work is broadly similar, or where pay is based on the results of a job evaluation scheme' (Council of Ministers, 1974b). It is this statement that left the Government with an understanding that the provisions of the Equal Pay Act would be in line with the directive.

The European Parliament fully supported the proposals for a new directive on equal pay. Indeed, it had been urging the Community for many years to work towards introducing new measures to implement equal pay fully. The Parliament had been critical of the slow progress in the application of equal pay in member states and was growing impatient at the lack of progress made. It was equally critical of overt forms of discrimination that were evident from changing wage groups and one-sided collectively agreed rates of pay for men and women. Parliament was clear that further steps were needed to be taken to achieve equal pay that went beyond the framework of existing legislation since unequal pay was a superficial expression of an old problem under new social and economic conditions.

However, the Council failed to incorporate Parliament's opinion in a way that substantially changed the nature and tone of the directive. This left the Parliament feeling that its role and influence had been circumvented in such an important area and like the Commission it was frustrated as to its lack of influence in the Council of Ministers. The final directive was much weaker than the original directive proposed by the Commission. It is evident that patriarchy played an important role in watering down some of the more controversial parts of the directive, where it was clear that member governments were not going to extend women's rights beyond what was acceptable at the national level.

The 1975 Equal Pay Directive extended equal pay and in the last event sought the 'approximation', rather than the 'harmonisation', of equal pay laws in member states. Despite the opposition in principle to equal pay for work of equal value from the UK, Danish and German delegations, who preferred the more limited definition of equal pay for equal work, the concept was introduced into the directive. The directive clarified the scope of equal pay to include the removal of discrimination in the drawing up of job classification schemes and from laws, regulations or administrative provisions. Employees were given the right to take legal action against their employers and to protection against dismissal if such actions were taken.

Although the introduction of the directive was a breakthrough, its implementation was not as swift as had been anticipated. The Commission had an important strategic role in monitoring legal compliance with the directive and used this power to force several member states to adopt the directive at a legal level. In its 1979 report on the implementation of the directive, the Commission found that although some progress had been made, only two member states, Italy and Ireland (whose legislation was framed on the directive), had fully implemented it.

In 1979 infringement proceedings were initiated against Belgium, Denmark, Luxembourg, Germany, France, The Netherlands and the UK, who had all failed to implement the directive. However, they were dropped against most member states as they voluntarily amended their own national legislation to bring it in line with the directive. For instance, in France, Luxembourg and Belgium this led to the removal of head-of-household allowances, and in The Netherlands to the extension of equal pay for work of equal value in the public sector. The UK and Germany were forced to amend their legislation after rulings in the European Court of Justice. Appendix 4 gives more information about the effect of these infringement proceedings on member states.

The infringements proceedings were necessary as it became clear that member states were not acting voluntarily to implement the directive. In this climate the Commission used its strategic role to promote equal pay through consultation with the 'social partners' and other relevant organisations in important discussions about policy. One initiative on indirect discrimination proved ill-fated when employers' organisations refused to discuss the issue with trade unions (Commission of the EC, 1981). They argued that it was not the job of the Commission to institute a European-wide system of job classification on indirect discrimination. Although the Commission's initiative was unsuccessful, it did have the effect of widening the debate about pay discrimination.

With the passing of the 1975 Directive, it became increasingly apparent that equal pay could do little to tackle women's inequalities in the labour market (European Parliament, 1976). Equal pay alone fails to address the problems of restricted opportunities open to women in the labour market, training and promotion, familial ideologies, sexual divisions and trade union and employer attitudes. These require fundamental changes in social attitudes towards women, a recognition of the sexual division of labour and the inherent gains that employers and men make from women's unequal position in the labour market. The recognition of these deeper structural problems led to the need for new EC provisions.

Equal treatment directive

In 1976 a directive on equal treatment was passed. Like the directive
on equal pay this directive had its roots in the 1974 Social Action
Programme. It sought to establish equality of treatment between men
and women with respect to access to employment, training and
promotion, and working conditions. It makes it illegal for member
states to discriminate directly or indirectly against women, particularly
regarding family and marital status. The negotiations for the directive,
in the Council of Ministers, were fraught with delays, revisions and
attempts to water down some of the more radical provisions, relating
to family responsibilities, as were the negotiations for the Equal Pay
Directive. Catherine Hoskyns (1986) has shown how 'The history of
these negotiations clearly illustrates the way in which institutionalized
patriarchy operates the political process' (p. 271).

The directive has been implemented in all member states, at least in
law. However, it was necessary for the Commission to issue infringement proceedings to force this implementation. Of particular importance is that the European Court of Justice, in the case of *Marshall* v.
Southampton and South-West Hampshire Health Authority, in 1986,
ruled that the directive was directly applicable in member states. This
has had the effect of widening the scope of the directive and has forced
the UK to change its law to comply with the Court's ruling.

Directive on equality in social security

A directive on equality in social security was passed in 1978.
Harmonisation of social security has been an important focus of EC
social policy, to ensure compatibility between the national laws of
member states, necessary to free movement of labour within the
Community. It is not surprising that social security was targeted as
an area in which the principle of equality could be applied.

However, the final form of the directive was also significantly
watered down by the Council of Ministers. Certain benefits, notably
those derived from occupational schemes, were excluded from its
scope. The Belgian and Italian delegations argued that occupational
benefits should be included, to avoid inequalities resulting in occupational and state benefits. This view was not upheld in the final
directive, although the Council of Ministers gave a commitment to
introduce a directive on occupational social security within two years.
The directive provides for the equalisation of social security benefits

for men and women and covers sickness, invalidity, retirement, industrial injury and occupational disease and unemployment. Its effect has been minimised by a very long implementation period of six years, requested by The Netherlands and the UK. The directive is narrow in scope and has not been far-reaching. It was never intended to ensure full equality in social security or the desegregation of social security benefits, argued for by many women throughout the EC. However, its effects have been felt in a number of ways. For example, in 1986 the European Court of Justice extended the scope of social security in the UK, to enable married women to claim the Invalid Care Allowance.

Training and education

It is clear that patterns of women's pay and employment will not improve to any great extent so long as women remain segregated from men in low-paid and low-skilled jobs. The opening up of jobs traditionally held by men has been encouraged on a small scale by the Community. In 1977 a directive was passed on the European Social Fund and gave a specific priority to training women over the age of 25 years who were re-entering the labour market after childrearing.

Education is another area where the Commission attempted to promote a climate for the removal of inequalities between men and women. The Commission's communication on the introduction of the Education Action Programme proposed in 1978 that equal educational and training opportunities should be open to girls and women. However, education has remained outside the scope of the EC competence and it is only at the level of exchanges of information and non-binding statements that the EC has been able to have an influence (Commission of the EC, 1978).

Despite a lot of progress in this stage it is evident that the Council of Ministers was fairly naive about the degree of incrementalism that was creeping into the women's policy. It failed to see the implications of broadening its scope in the long term. In making reference to the 1975 Directive the UK permanent representative to the Council of Ministers argued that 'I don't think we would have agreed to this measure if we had known about the implications that it would have to the government now over the Equal Pay Act' (interview, Brussels, 1981). This naivety was soon recognised as the EC moved into the latter part of this second stage.

It is evident that the Commission, in particular, faced a number of problems. It was extremely difficult to measure progress towards equal pay, since information given to the Commission was based on national government reports. It was even more difficult for the Commission to measure any such progress in relation to the position of women in the labour market. However, pressure from the European Parliament and a more sophisticated method of collecting statistics led to more information on the actual position of women than was evident in the 1960s and early 1970s. Again, it was virtually impossible for the Commission to point directly to wage discrimination and the violation of the principle, since equal pay is a matter for national governments to implement. This stage of development highlighted one further problem for the Commission. This was that it had little control over the changing economic and political priorities of member states. It was felt from the initial enthusiasm generated by the Social Action Programme and the later reluctance by member states to implement its provisions. It was also evident as the oil crisis and recession took priority over an increase in the budget of the Social Action Programme. These changing economic and political priorities became clearer as policies entered the third phase of development.

Nevertheless, the legal instruments introduced gradually led to the development, outlook and thinking on equality between men and women. They helped to construct a better understanding, and a change in attitude towards the role of women in the labour market. It is perhaps for this reason that the Council of Ministers was to become more reluctant to extend the frontiers of this approach beyond the scope of that achieved in the second stage of development.

THIRD STAGE: FROM LEGISLATION TO DIALOGUE, 1978–86

The growing awareness of the social context of women's employment increased the pressure to widen policy initiatives after 1978. However, this was met with an uncertain economic and political environment and, in the event, fewer binding legal measures were introduced. Economic decline and a growing divergence between member states' economic performance meant that progress on women's policies was politically controversial. The early 1980s saw growing rates of unemployment and economic crisis hitting women and it was clear that EC policy to promote women's rights at work had done little to prevent a serious and deteriorating situation. This has to be seen against the background of the fact that political will to extend women's rights was only evident in two member states, France and Greece. A great deal of disillusionment about the EC's role was expressed during the early part of this stage. It was marked by some member states, particularly the UK, asserting national sovereignty above Community progress and restricting the impact of this policy development.

Women became much more involved in lobbying the EC in the 1980s, particularly through the creation of women's networks outside the EC institutional structure. This was a response to the growing awareness and importance attached to EC initiatives by many women across Europe. There was also a significant increase in the numbers of women consulted by the EC institutions. Gaiotti de Baise, MEP, argued that:

> women are coming to be one of the social groups with the greatest interest in the furtherance of the integration of the Community; they have strengthened their solidarity beyond frontiers, basing it on an institution, and using official international instruments. (European Parliament, 1984a)

While pressure from women was taken seriously by the Commission and the Parliament, it was met with resistance in the Council of Ministers. The emphasis in this stage shifted to the consolidation of the legislative gains of the 1970s to ensure that member states fulfilled their obligations under EC law. In the third stage the Commission relied less on government reports and more on the use of independent experts to monitor progress. Coupled with this the Parliament's and the Commission's roles in promoting and developing policies on women's rights became more visible. These will now be looked at in turn.

The European Parliament and its role in the promotion of women's rights

During this stage the European Parliament became more active in promoting policies for women and pressurising the Council and

Commission into action. It no longer saw the promotion of women's rights as something that was to be left to 'women's organisations and progressive feminists' (European Parliament, 1983, p. 10). For some political groups women's rights were central policy and electoral issues. In particular, the socialist group saw itself as having a vital role to play in becoming 'one of the most effective lobbies on women's issues, especially at this time when, under pressure from the Right, the Commission is increasingly being forced to backtrack on new proposals to help women' (British Labour Group, 1984, p. 1).

In 1981 this led the Ad Hoc Committee on Women's Rights to call for new policies that went beyond the scope of the directives (European Parliament, 1981a). This generated a new level of support for women and led to the setting up of a special Committee of Inquiry into the situation of women in Europe. In 1984 the Committee reported that the situation of women in Europe had deteriorated. Concern was expressed over growing unemployment amongst women, the threat of further job losses through technological change, cuts in social services, and a heavier burden of domestic responsibilities and caring by women. They reiterated the urgent need for policies that were more flexible and wider in scope.

It was evident also that EC policies had not improved the situation of women across Europe. For instance, the Committee criticised the European Social Fund for failing to benefit girls and women fully, despite the effect of the special budget item on women's training projects. The Committee was equally critical of the way in which the equal pay and equal treatment directives had been implemented and their failure to reduce the concentration of women in the lowest-paid sectors. They warned that the equal pay and equal treatment directives were under threat if they were not implemented and backed up by new actions. Parliament argued that it was vital to introduce new measures to integrate women fully into the labour market, through the reorganisation of working time and positive action:

> There is a danger that the present economic crisis will aggravate the weakness and subordination of the female labour force, driving increasing numbers of women into the black economy and precarious forms of employment, where they are vulnerable to exploitation; there is also the danger that it will block the plans or present initiatives to improve the level of education or training within the female workforce and encourage retraining. (European Parliament, 1984a)

Although the Committee was divided along party political lines, its 1983 report showed the concern and importance attached to women's rights in a worsening economic climate (European Parliament, 1983). Some members of the Committee questioned the widening scope of EC policy on women, seeing many of the actions recommended by the Women's Committee as extending its brief too far. For instance, Dame Shelagh Roberts (British Conservative Group) commented that the Committee's scope had been too wide and too general. There had been a 'proliferation of the agenda', and by looking at problems of women in the third world, for example, had moved too far away from the central purpose of the Committee. She had found many of the suggested actions to be 'unreasonable' (interview, Strasbourg, 1983).

The European Parliament had certainly become an important force in pushing for a wider and more substantial EC policy, which concentrated on some of the structural problems associated with women's pay and employment. In this respect, the Parliament has been an important initiator of new ideas for policy and an effective source of support for the Commission.

The role of the Commission

The Commission remained committed to extending policies for women during this stage of development. This resulted in a much greater awareness of EC activities by women throughout the Community, and the impact that this could have on their own domestic legislation. The Commission was keen to develop new Community instruments and reacted positively to the pressure coming both from the European Parliament and from women outside the Community. Speaking in the European Parliament, Commissioner Richards stated that:

there is no reason why women should bear more than their proportionate and fair share of the burdens imposed by the economic crisis. The actions and initiatives the Commission is taking at the moment in this field are intended to counteract this tendency which is contrary to the provisions and spirit of Community legislation and commitments on equal treatment. (European Parliament, 1984a)

However, the Council of Ministers showed a marked reluctance to agree to binding measures. In this light the Commission was forced to constrain its role, as Commissioner Richards stated in an interview in 1984:

> There is no point in presenting a radical proposal to the Council of Ministers that we know would not get through, it would be a waste of ours and their time, no matter what our feelings may be in this regard. (Strasbourg, 1984)

Nevertheless, the Commission continued to develop new initiatives and a new Action Programme on the Promotion of Equal Opportunities for Women 1982–5 was passed by the Council of Ministers in 1982. This was largely a result of the persuasion in the Council of Ministers of Yvette Roudy, the French Minister for Women's Rights. She had been actively promoting new women's policies in France and had previously been President of the European Parliament's Ad Hoc Committee on Women's Rights.

However, many of the actions were watered down by the Council of Ministers, they were vague and failed to propose binding instruments to implement the actions. As a result many of the actions were left to the goodwill of member states to implement. The UK actively sought to block any further initiatives in this area, at a time when the Conservative Government was neither in favour of extending women's rights in any substantive way, nor wanting to pursue a wider goal of European integration.

The four-year Action Programme, 1982–5

The Action Programme sought to strengthen women's rights and implement equal opportunities for women, but was limited in the legal weight attached to it. It did, however, lead to the passing of two new directives that had been promised in 1978. A brief look at the effects and results of the actions will show that Community policy in this area had moved away from the relative consensus of the extension of Community law in the 1970s, to national concerns and hostility towards Community action in the 1980s. This is evident in the failure of the Council of Ministers to agree to pass a directive on parental leave. The first action required the Commission 'to reinforce and monitor the practical application of the Directives in the member states, their progress and interpretation given to community measures at national level with particular attention to indirect discrimination'. This led to the formation of a network of experts to monitor

Community legislation in 1984. The network has been a particularly important lever to the Commission and has been highly critical of the implementation and scope of the directives:

> If the directives were designed to remove individual injustices, then to a fair extent they have succeeded. If on the other hand they were designed to reform the labour market so as to de-segregate it, rid it of sex bias and the resulting distortions, and introduce complete equality of opportunity in an individual, economic and structural sense, then they have not yet delivered the necessary results . . . there is an important need for the clarification of the political objectives of the Community in this area. (Von Prondzynski, 1987, p. 55)

The network recommended new legislation on the reversal of the burden of proof in equality cases, the extension and clarification of indirect discrimination, positive action and that more research should be undertaken.

The four-year Action Programme also led to the passing of new directives in the area of occupational social security and social security for self-employed women. These had been promised with the passing of the 1978 equality in social security directive and the Council of Ministers was obliged to stick to its commitments. After three years of tortuous negotiation, a new directive on occupational social security was adopted by the Council on 5 June 1986. The final form of the directive was substantially watered down from the original proposal put forward by the Commission.

Particular opposition to this directive came from the UK, who insisted that only with more restricted provisions would agreement to the directive be reached. The outcome was that exemptions, permitting companies to set different benefits for men and women, was maintained. Moreover, the directive was given a long phasing-in period, with the date for implementation set at 1993.

The introduction of equal treatment to self-employed women and women in agriculture, especially regarding pay and social security, was another area that led to controversial and heated discussions in the Council of Ministers. There was, at least, a level of agreement that such a provision would be necessary to back up the 1978 Social Security Directive. A directive was finally passed in 1986.

A more controversial proposed directive on parental leave and leave for family reasons was first placed before the Council of Ministers in

1983, followed by an amended proposal in 1984. Parental leave had already been introduced in a number of Scandinavian countries, France, Italy and Germany, and gave the working mother or father the right to leave in the event of a newborn baby or to care for a sick child or other relative. This was the first attempt by the Commission to introduce a policy that would have a direct effect on family responsibilities. The proposed directive argued that both parents should have the right to take at least three months' leave, to be taken at any time until their child was 2 years old, or five years' in the case of adopted or handicapped children. The proposal also contained a number of safeguards including the reinstatement of the worker to the same or equivalent job, and the crediting of leave for the purposes of social security benefits.

The UK government consistently opposed this directive, on the grounds that the costs to employers would outweigh the benefits. Lobbying by employers and opposition from Conservatives in the European Parliament stressed the need for parental leave to be enacted voluntarily, in order that small firms would not be penalised, although overall the Parliament did support the proposal (European Parliament, 1984b). Despite several attempts to reach agreement by watering down the proposals to exclude small businesses, firms in difficulty and parents whose partners were out of work, the UK has continued to block the directive.

Other aspects of the Action Programme included a large number of new provisions with no legal enforcement attached to them. These included a survey on the provisions of legal redress in member states and reports on the taxation of working women and the provision of national and EC protective legislation that fell outside the scope of the Equal Treatment Directive. However, no attempt was made to introduce new initiatives that would enforce better systems of legal redress or protective legislation. A memorandum recommending the independent taxation of men and women was issued, but had no legal weight.

A further study was carried out on the protection of women during pregnancy and motherhood. This was the first step in the Commission's long-term aim of harmonising provisions throughout the EC. Legislative action was seen to be inappropriate at this stage. It was clear that the attitude of the Council of Ministers to further extensions of rights for women in this area would not favour a firm legal provision. Harmonisation was particularly opposed by the UK who was more concerned at the time to reduce, rather than increase, protection during pregnancy and motherhood. It had no intention of improving provision particularly in line with countries like France and Belgium, whose protection was of a high standard. One particularly important new initiative was in the area of positive action. This was an issue that had been receiving attention from trade unions and women's organisations throughout the EC. This was due to a realisation that legislation failed to remove some of the deep-seated prejudicial attitudes towards women's roles. Positive action attempts to give positive encouragement to women applying for particular jobs and taking up particular forms of training, especially in non-traditional areas. A recommendation was passed in 1984 and Community action was confined to studies and seminars, making it little more than educational.

Other actions led to further studies, seminars and information exchanges that were aimed at changing attitudes. These included integration into working life (regarding new technology), enhancing vocational choices for girls and women, desegregation of employment, equal treatment in employment and training for migrant women, and the sharing of occupational, family and social responsibilities. The Commission actively encouraged the use of feminist research to develop these policy initiatives, not least in the area of positive action.

The Action Programme in its final form was one with little budgetary and political backing from the Council of Ministers. Its impact has been little more than that of promoting social dialogue, kept alive by the Commission's continued persistence. Overall it had a limited impact:

> Using economic necessity as a pretext they (the Council of Ministers) have all too often ignored their commitment and actually undermined existing achievement. . . . They have on the whole failed to implement any of the major provisions of the programme. (CREW, vol. 6, no. 7)

Whilst supporting many of the actions, the Commission was frequently left in a powerless position. This was a result of the Council of Ministers either blocking or seriously undermining proposals for legislative action. Many of the initiatives and actions that were passed in the resolution were left, in the last event, to the goodwill and voluntarism of member states to implement. However, the Commission concluded, in its 1985 report on the implementation of the Action Programme, that despite the limitations in implementing the actions in member states it was 'having a very positive and stimulating effect on the development of action to promote equal opportunities for women'.

Second Action Programme, 1986–90

In order to avoid losing momentum in this field and responding to the European Parliament's 1984 resolution, calling for a comprehensive and wide-ranging policy, a second medium-term programme (1986–90) was proposed by the Commission in 1985. This was designed to follow up some of the actions initiated by the 1982–5 Action Programme, to ensure that initiatives were not lost and to introduce a more wide-ranging policy.

As with the first Action Programme, the actions planned did not involve any legislative impact. Instead they concentrated on education, information, discussions and seminars. As well as pursuing initiatives in the first Action Programme, the Commission was also responding to new economic and social changes, notably in the area of technological change.

Other EC initiatives

Other initiatives falling outside the Action Programmes received little support in the Council of Ministers. Initiatives such as the Commission's *Guidelines for Action to Combat Women's Unemployment* saw the Council of Ministers dragging its feet, as many member governments were implementing policies that continued to erode women's rights.

Heated and protracted discussions were held on the reduction and reorganisation of working time. This initiative has been seen, on the one hand, as a measure of employment creation, and on the other hand, as a means to introduce more flexible working time for women and to enable both men and women to share more domestic tasks. The Community only went as far as discussing a proposal for a recommendation, which is non-binding and lacks the legal weight of a directive.

Draft directive on voluntary part-time work

A further proposed directive on voluntary part-time work, in 1982, was also blocked in the Council of Ministers. This was the result of a very effective employers' lobby which won strong support from the UK. The draft directive on voluntary part-time work was one of the most significant pieces of proposed legislation since the 1975 Equal Pay Directive. It was also one of the more controversial areas of EC policy to have come before the Council of Ministers. It was initiated as part of a series of measures on the reorganisation of working time, which marked a substantial shift in Commission policy. This was a result of the growing concern with the state of employment throughout the Community.

Overall, it aimed to give part-time work the same status as full-time work. It required that there would be no discrimination between full- and part-time workers regarding pay, fringe benefits, social security benefits, employment protection and conditions of employment in written agreements. The purpose of the draft directive was three-fold: to encourage part-time work and thus reduce unemployment, to make part-time work more attractive by improving its status, and to complement existing directives on equal pay and equal treatment for men and women.

The UK Government was the only member government to give outright opposition (Department of Employment, 1983a). In 1982 a written reply to a parliamentary question saw Michael Alison, Minister of State at the time, defending employers' interests:

> The Government believes that part-time work should be encour-aged, but that the draft EEC directive would introduce undesirable rigidities into the labour market and generally decrease the oppor-tunities for part-time work.

Strong support was given to the directive by the French Govern-ment, which had introduced domestic legislation similar to that being proposed in the directive. Indeed, France urged that the directive should contain stronger provisions than those set out in the draft. Reservations were expressed by the Danish, German and Irish delegations, who were prepared to commit themselves to a weaker directive. The Danish reservations related to the fact that no employ-ment protection legislation existed for any employees in Denmark, and the delegation was therefore concerned not to give the right to non-discrimination to part-time workers and not to full-time workers. The German delegation (in a similar vein to their negotiations over the

Equal Pay Directive) expressed its desire to see such issues dealt with in collective bargaining.

In September 1982, the UK House of Lords Select Committee on European Legislation published its report on *Voluntary Part-Time Work* (House of Lords, 1982). It concluded that there was a need to protect the rights of part-time workers and that there was a strong case for introducing further protective measures for them. The Committee argued that the Government had been mistaken in opposing the draft directive in the Council of Ministers, and urged it to seek radical amendments, rather than opposing it outright. Nevertheless the UK continued to oppose the directive, despite the fact that a new draft directive was issued in 1983 that included the employers' defence.

A directive to protect the rights of temporary workers suffered a similar fate in the Council of Ministers, and like the part-time work directive, it too was vetoed by the UK for the same reasons.

As a result of these developments there was a movement away from firm legislative provisions towards dialogue and retrenchment. The extent of dialogue was evident from the wide ranging use of studies, seminars and blocked legislation in the Council of Ministers. More time was spent, during this stage, in devising ways in which legislation could be obstructed or introduced by voluntary methods than was evident during the second stage. Nevertheless, the Commission and the Parliament kept issues on the agenda and created a climate of opinion outside the Community sufficient to maintain effective pressure.

Such was the opposition of the Council of Ministers to furthering the role of the Community in the area of women's rights that the Commission was forced into a position of compromise. This was asserted in much stronger terms with the appointment of a new Commissioner for Social Affairs, Manuel Marin, who in 1986 argued that 'The European Commission may abandon its effort to promote women's equality in the face of continued opposition by governments'. He was clear that ministers 'do not want an EEC policy in favour of women. They are not interested in it' (CREW, vol. 7, no. 7, p. 13)

CONCLUSION

This chapter has shown how women's policies developed between 1957 and 1986 in three distinct stages of development. Each stage has responded to differing political, economic and social objectives which were met with growing pressure and lobbying from women. In the first stage the introduction of equal pay for equal work in Article 119 established the basis for further policy initiatives that were taken up in the second and third stages. While the second stage (up to 1978) saw the commitment to introduce new directives, the third stage (up to 1986) saw this falter as the Council of Ministers sought to restrict enactments beyond voluntary agreements. This was seen most clearly in the failure to agree and adopt directives on part-time work, temporary work and parental leave. Nevertheless a wider policy framework was sought from women in the member states of the EC and from the Parliament and the Commission. Without the political pressure of a growing women's lobby it is doubtful that the measures introduced after 1978 would have seen the light of day.

6 How has EC Policy Affected Women in the UK? A Case Study of the Equal Pay Directive

If the EC is to develop policies that will positively benefit women's employment in the single market, then there is a need to ensure that policies are implemented in an effective way in member states. This chapter looks at how the 1975 Equal Pay Directive has been interpreted by and implemented in the UK. From this it is apparent that there are problems in relying on national goodwill to implement policies with the spirit in which they were intended to take effect. The under-representation of women's interests in policy-making and the over-representation of patriarchal interests means that there is no guarantee that policies will be implemented in a way that positively benefits women.

THE EQUAL PAY ACT AND EC LAW

Article 119, which overrides national law and which the national courts have been bound to recognise and protect, gives women the right to equal pay. The direct applicability of Article 119 was established in practice in 1971 in *Defrenne* v. *Sabena*. Since then a number of important cases have been referred to the European Court of Justice for clarification and these have had the effect of broadening the scope of equal pay in the UK in a number of important ways (see Appendix 6).

In contrast to Article 119, the 1975 directive has had to be implemented through legislative change in the UK. It was not until 1984 that this was finally achieved.

The European Commission first began proceedings against the UK in March 1979 on the grounds that the Equal Pay Act failed to implement the 1975 directive, particularly in comparing jobs of equal value. The only means of achieving equal value was through job evaluation and since this was not compulsory under the Equal Pay Act, the Commission argued that the terms of the directive were not being fully implemented. Neither was there anything empowering employers to carry out job evaluation studies, nor an outside body to which women could turn for an assessment of equal value.

However, the Government consistently maintained that the Commission's accusations were unfounded. It argued that equal pay for work of equal value had been logically and practically interpreted in the Act, in a way that had not been achieved in other member states. The Government was clear that compulsory job evaluation was not required in the directive and argued that in the absence of a job evaluation scheme, there were no other mechanisms that could be introduced to implement equal value. Nevertheless, the Commission was not convinced by the Government's arguments and in 1980 delivered a 'reasoned opinion' inviting the Government to comply within two months. The Government failed to do this and in 1981 the UK was taken to the European Court of Justice.

It was clear that the European Court of Justice took this case seriously and, in its judgment, the Court upheld the Commission's case (Case 61/81). It argued that the Equal Pay Act failed to provide the machinery and an appropriate administrative channel through which women could claim equal pay for work of equal value. The UK, therefore, had to establish an authority that could determine equal value, thereby ensuring that employers no longer had the sole responsibility for determining the exact nature of equal pay.

Although the Commission knew that the Government sought to restrict the change as much as possible it was aware that the final product should be left to the national parliamentary process. Officials in the Commission felt that they were too distant from and had too few contacts with officials in member states to influence implementation. As a result:

> The real impact of Community law on national policy is obscured and minimised by national governments (not just the UK). Governments don't want to be seen by the electorate to have constraints and limitations imposed on them. (Interview, Colin Robertson, EC Legal Service, 1983).

AMENDING THE EQUAL PAY ACT

The possibility of a new Act was outruled from the start, despite growing pressure for new legislation (Sex Equality Bill 1983, EOC,

1981). Instead the Government chose to use the procedure for
amending UK law on the basis of EC law. It is a simple procedure,
made by introducing a regulation for an amending order under Section
2(2) of the European Communities Act 1972. This procedure was
heavily criticised since no time was allowed for debate or the possibility
of placing further amendments before Parliament. It gave the Government the opportunity to introduce legislation that was not in keeping
with the spirit of EC law. The National Council for Civil Liberties
(Rights of Women Unit) (1982) was one of several organisations
concerned with the effects of such legislation on an amendment to the
Equal Pay Act: 'This procedure bypasses the normal Parliamentary
procedure on Bills. It therefore does not allow full democratic
discussion from which the best amendment could emerge to make the
concept of equal pay for work of equal value most effective' (p. 2). The
Government's role was confined to fulfilling EC obligations, and
avoiding an embarrassment, at the European level, for failing to do
this. It left untouched the broader, more far-reaching changes that were
suggested by a number of pressure groups. Proposals for amending the
Equal Pay Act were circulated for consultation on two occasions,
through its original specifications and its draft Equal Value Order.

The Government's original specifications

The original specifications for amending the Act, issued on 12 August
1982, were highly complex and proposed that equal value claims
should be dealt with by the industrial tribunals (Department of
Employment, 1982). If conciliation failed, the industrial tribunal
would attempt to deal with the claim as 'like work' or 'work rated
as equivalent' under the Equal Pay Act. If neither of these applied, the
tribunal would then go on to consider a claim under equal value, by
introducing a job evaluation study. A time limit of between six and
nine months was recommended for reporting back, and, if the job
evaluation showed that the jobs were of an equal value there might be
no need for further reference to the tribunal. If this was the case and
there was no genuine material difference, modification to the appli-
cant's contract could be made.

However, in cases where there was no agreement or cooperation in
the introduction of a job evaluation study, it was proposed that an
independent assessor would be appointed to evaluate the jobs. The
assessor's report would form the basis by which the tribunal reached
its decision.

Widespread criticisms were made of the proposals on the grounds that they were unclear and unworkable. It was mainly the organised and well-established groups that responded to the Government's consultations at this stage.

Much of the divergence of views as how best to implement the European Court's decision rested on the conflict between which body should handle equal value claims and the methods for assessing claims. Further differences existed in the envisaged role of the independent assessors. The Equal Opportunities Commission argued that it was necessary to have a specialist group of people, with expert knowledge and experience of job evaluation, in order that the proposed changes to the Act could work in practice. If industrial tribunals lacked expertise and insight in the administration of the Equal Pay Act, then the Equal Opportunities Commission saw that it would be impossible for them to handle complicated legislation of this nature. For the Equal Opportunities Commission, this expertise should be left to a group of 'equality officers', akin to those employed in Ireland.

The draft equal value order

On 16 February 1983, the Government published its second set of proposals for consultation (Department of Employment, 1983b, 1983c, 1983d). The draft order represented a considerable simplification of the original specification, having 'retreated from its first more complex and indeed unworkable scheme' (National Council for Civil Liberties, 1982). The Government took more notice of the Confederation of British Industry than it did of any other group that it consulted. This is not surprising since it was clear that the Government was reluctant to amend the Act in the first place, given its close alliances with employers. The order proposed to bring legislation into force in twelve months. Such a long gap in enforcement was clearly not within the spirit of the European Court's judgment, and the recommendations for an immediate implementation of the provisions were ignored.

This stage of consultation saw a larger number of groups promoting and representing women's interests. Many argued that while providing a technical solution to the court's judgment, the provisions failed to create the machinery that would enable women to claim equal pay for equal value in a practical and realistic way. Equal pay for work of equal value has the potential to break down job segregation and enable women who have no man working alongside them to make claims. However, in practice, the draft order placed severe limitations on this. According to the National Council for Civil Liberties (Rights of Women Group) (1982): 'The Equal Pay Act has been criticised for being difficult to understand and operate. The Draft Order does nothing to improve this . . . the Order is almost incomprehensible. The Equal Pay Act no longer has any effect on women's low pay' (p. 1). It was further criticised as being complex, long-winded, confusing and showing no real commitment to promoting the concept of equal value in an effective and realistic way. This was heightened by the fact that tribunals would be given more incentive to dismiss equal value claims than hear them.

The Equal Pay and Opportunity Campaign (1983) was in no doubt that the character of the draft order was 'so unreasonably weighted against the claimant that its disincentive element is counter-productive to the objective . . . [it would not] have the effect of enabling those women whom the legislation currently fails to help to successfully claim equal pay for work of equal value, (p. 3). The draft order was also criticised for its failure to implement the provisions of the directive in collective bargaining and collective agreements. Likewise there was no mention of fulfilling the provisions of the directive which requires that employees should be informed of the provisions contained in the directive.

The fact that an equal value claim could only be made if unsuccessful under the criteria of 'like work' or if the job had not been evaluated as the same as a man's in a job evaluation study posed a number of drawbacks. First, if the woman's work and that of her comparator had been rated differently under a job evaluation study, an equal value claim would not be permitted unless the woman could make a comparison with the work of another man who was not covered under the study. Second, as with other equal pay claims, it became impossible to make a claim on the basis of two alternative headings, for example, equal value and/or like work. Third, no clarity was given as to whether an equal value claim could be brought under the 'like work' heading. Therefore, it would be possible for a claim to be made under like work and then be dismissed without hearing a case for equal value.

Unlike equal pay cases, if the tribunal found 'no reasonable grounds' for an equal value case it could dismiss the case, without even hearing all the facts. This was a particularly important part of the order, given the novel nature of equal value and the potential it has for challenging traditional views on the value attributed to women's work. Tribunals, unaccustomed to the concept and philosophy of equal value, could dismiss a case as having 'no reasonable grounds' precisely because of a failure to challenge the value and worth of women's jobs. This was particularly likely since little or no guidance was given in the order as to the meaning of equal value. Clearly tribunals, who have in the past been shown to be rigid in their decisions on equal pay cases, are unlikely to be made up of members who would be able to make a conceptual shift in the way that they work and think, to allow for the wider notion of equal value to be taken seriously.

Further shortcomings were evident in the procedures which enable an employer to prove, before any evidence is heard on equal value, that a difference in pay is due to a 'material difference'. This provision had more disadvantages than under any other UK employment legislation. This is because an employer is able to prove a 'material difference' before the case is heard and where prepared facts and figures of wage structures, to justify a difference in pay, can be presented. The actual burden of proof would rest on the claimant, posing a serious hurdle and disincentive to claims being made. If a woman could not show that a difference in pay was due to sex, and this would be extremely difficult to prove, particularly where indirect discrimination had taken place, the case would then be dismissed.

Under these circumstances, it was clear that few women would win cases under these provisions, which were heavily weighted in favour of the employer. Moreover, it was unclear as to what could constitute a 'genuine material difference'. This could be loosely interpreted, if, for instance, part-time work or shorter working hours could form a justification for a material difference.

The role of 'independent experts' was also addressed in the draft order. The Government, however, rejected earlier proposals for equality officers. Little or no guidance was given on the envisaged role or expertise of the independent experts and no code of practice established, as had been suggested by the Equal Opportunities Commission (EOC, 1983a, 1983b). This led to doubts as to how far the investigation would be carried out in a way that was sympathetic to the principle of equal value and free from sex bias.

The final decision of a case was in the hands of the industrial tribunals and while a tribunal would not be able to determine whether work was of an equal value, unless it received a report from an independent expert, the report was not regarded as binding. The length of the procedure up to this stage posed many disincentives for a claim to be continued, particularly if a woman is taking a case independent of trade union or other support. One reason for women not taking cases to industrial tribunals is the fear of the financial burden of losing a case. The order provided that women would have to pay employers' legal costs where cases were lost. No provision was made for claims that made reference to a hypothetical male worker or a man working in a different establishment, as exists in other European countries. This restricted the scope for comparisons in an already segregated labour market.

The draft order enabled the Equal Opportunities Commission, under the Sex Discrimination Act, to require an employer not to act in breach of the right to equal pay for work of equal value, through use of formal investigations. It was highly questionable as to how far it should, on the one hand, be expected to carry out this role if its size and budget were not increased and, on the other hand, if it was appropriate for it to do so.

The Government postponed the date that the order came before the House of Lords, for fear that it would not be passed. It was strongly criticised by Lord Denning in the House of Lords (1983):

> While the enactments of the Treaty and the directives are reasonably clear and can be understood, our own enactments are deplorable . . . Its tortuosity and complexity is beyond compare. No ordinary individual can understand it . . . no ordinary lawyer would be able to understand them. (cols 901–2)

There were equally forceful criticisms of the order in the House of Commons (1983), described by Mark Lennox-Boyd, MP, as 'legal gobbledegook'. Anthony Lestor, QC (1983), sums up much of this thinking:

> these proposals do not give proper effect to the principle of equal pay for work of equal value. I have never seen more complicated, grotesquely complicated proposals. They are a kind of game of snakes and ladders with a lot of powerful snakes and some pathetic ladders. The whole game is weighted against women in favour of the employer . . . [the proposals] will be in breach of (European) Community law and they will be contrary to the fundamental principles of British justice. (p. 21)

The Equal Opportunities Commission was also clear that EC obligations were not being met and that this could lead to further protracted litigation in both the national and European courts (EOC, 1983b). The EC Commission's lack of power to affect and alter this implementation process remains a serious criticism of the impact of policy in practice. Although it was clear that Commission officials were unhappy about the mechanisms adopted to introduce equal value, there was a reluctance to issue further infringement proceedings and to embark on what would have been a highly controversial and lengthy case.

The Government's response to the criticisms

It is apparent that criticisms of the draft order had a positive effect in making some changes to the Government's final Order. This was evident in a statement made in the House of Commons by Michael Allison, the then Minister of State for Employment. It was recommended that a number of changes be made. First, the burden of proof would no longer rest on the woman. Second, women were given the right to claim equal value in a job that had previously been covered by a job evaluation study. Third, the regulations would come into force on 1 January 1984, giving a shorter implementation period than had been initially proposed.

The role of pressure groups had evidently been successful in removing some of the more controversial proposals. There is no doubt that this pressure secured, at least in part, that women's interests were reflected in the policy process.

The resulting amendment is an example of how, on the one hand, the EC attempted to enforce the application of a directive, while on the other hand, it was powerless to ensure that it is applied in a way that meets not only with the letter of EC law but also with the spirit of it. This shows the severe shortcomings of the EC's policy of equal pay that is heavily reliant on the goodwill of member states over which the Commission has little control. Nevertheless, the amendment would scarcely have been introduced had it not been for pressure from the EC. Pressure groups and other interest organisations were quick to take up the initiative from the Commission. It is evident that the EC was viewed as an important means of improving women's rights at work at a time when the Government was failing to do anything to improve women's position in the labour market.

EQUAL VALUE IN PRACTICE

Despite the shortcomings of the legislation, it became possible for pay structures to be challenged and reassessed in a way that had not been possible before. This was particularly important for women not working alongside men, for regrading and re-evaluating jobs and taking women out of the low pay ghetto. Of equal importance is that it became possible for the courts, unions and employers to reassess the value of women's work. However, the provisions failed to address the issue of occupational segregation, and therefore the under-valuation of women's work. For women with no male comparator in the same establishment there is no remedy.

The role of the tribunals and courts

A number of trade unions and the Equal Opportunities Commission have looked at ways to make full use of the amended legislation, and have actively encouraged women to make claims. However, the Equal Opportunities Commission stated in 1986 that the 'lengthy and costly procedures' involved in making a claim for equal value 'and the mere handful of women who have so far been successful in their claims offers little prospect of an early change to the situation' (EOC, 1986). However there has been a steady rise in the number of cases of equal pay reaching the tribunals, many of which have been equal value cases.

Table 6.1 shows that between 1984 and 1989 there were 1520 applications to industrial tribunals involving 413 employers. Some of these applications have included multiple applications, for instance

Table 6.1   Applications to industrial tribunals, 1984–9

Year	Applications
1984	229
1985	382
1986	366
1987	343
1988	90
1989	110
Total	1520

Source: Equal Opportunities Review, July/August 1990

from 1395 speech therapists in 1987 and 1115 employees of British Coal in 1986, Other multiple applications have been made by district health authorities, Lloyds Bank employees and Vauxhall Motors employees. The highest number of applications were made in 1985 and the numbers have continued to decline since then.

Equal value claims have proved very lengthy. In 1989 cases took an average of 17 months to be settled. Some cases have taken up to three years to reach the final decision in the tribunal and longer if the employer appeals. Other cases have often taken several years to reach a preliminary hearing. For instance, a claim by canteen workers from the National Union of Miners took over three years to reach a preliminary hearing. The length of cases has been increased by employers making much greater use of 'material difference defence' arguments in the tribunals. Likewise, further delays have been evident in the appointment of an independent assessor, which has sometimes taken up to two years. The complexity and length of the procedures on equal value has led the Employment Appeal Tribunal to suggest a quicker procedure and the Equal Opportunities Commission to draw up proposals to make the procedure fairer and quicker (EOC, 1989).

The expense of taking cases through the tribunals has meant that women can only lodge claims if supported by their unions or by the Equal Opportunities Commission. Both face financial crises and are limited in the amount of support they can offer.

It is evident from Table 6.2 that a small proportion of all cases are upheld by the tribunal, with a significant number of cases either being rejected or settled/withdrawn at an early stage. Cases that are settled or withdrawn are sometimes successful and have been a useful backdrop for unions in collective bargaining. However, there has been only a 15 per cent success rate of tribunal awards for equal value in the UK, compared to a much more favourable success rate in

Table 6.2   Outcome of equal value claims

	1988	1989	1990
Upheld by tribunal	13	20	25
Rejected by tribunal	18	24	46
Outstanding	34	36	25
On appeal	5	5	7
Settled/withdrawn	31	43	61

Source: Labour Research Department, June 1989 and June 1990.

Ireland of 95 per cent. Much of this has been related to the legislation being seriously undermined by narrow interpretations in the tribunals and courts. The lengthy tribunal process meant that only about 50 cases reached the 'independent expert' stage by the first half of 1988. Half of these cases had been through the independent expert stage, where eleven were deemed not to be of an equal value by the independent expert and fourteen were judged to be of an equal value. Of these, five were settled before the expert reported in favour of the women. In cases where the independent expert has reported, settlement in favour of the claimants has been the frequent outcome.

Case law

A number of claims for equal value have led to the development of important case law in the courts. Some of these cases have reached the House of Lords for final decisions. Appendix 5 lists the cases that have been important in establishing this in the UK.

The first successful, but nonetheless lengthy and controversial, case concerned that of a woman, Julie Hayward, a qualified cook, who was paid the canteen assistant's rate of pay (*Hayward* v. *Cammell Laird* (1984)). She claimed equal pay for work of equal value with painters, joiners and heating engineers working for the same company who had received equal training and yet were paid the skilled rate of pay. This case was particularly important because it established the first case law on equal value and was an important impetus to further claims and to subsequent tribunal decisions. EC law was used to establish that 'pay' included differences in hours of work, time rates as compared to piece rates, paid meal breaks, bonuses, overtime rates, paid holidays and benefits in kind.

Equally important was the case of *Pickstone* v. *Freemans plc* (1987). A claim for equal value was initially rejected in the Court of Appeal because a woman was already employed on work that was the same as that of a man, as well as being of an equal value to that of a man working in another job. However, the changes made to the Equal Pay Act as a result of EC law were used to override this decision in determining that such a situation should not debar a claim for equal value.

Another important, but unsuccessful, case was that of the sewing machinists at the Ford plant, Dagenham (*Neil and Others* v. *Ford Motor Company* (1988)). In 1967, women sewing machinists had been put into the new B grade, whilst skilled men enjoyed the pay of the skilled C grade. In 1968, the women went on strike to achieve regrading with the skilled men, and while they achieved a pay increase, failed to be regraded or to be recognised as skilled workers. The introduction of the Equal Pay Act failed to provide a remedy for the women. It was only in 1985, backed by their union, that they were able to make a claim for regrading under the amended Act. This was made on the basis that there had been a discriminatory job evaluation scheme. Their jobs were evaluated by an independent assessor to establish if grades B and C were of an equal value. The final decision of the tribunal dismissed the case, arguing that the previous job evaluation scheme had not been discriminatory. However, the women sewing machinists were later upgraded after the Advisory, Conciliation and Arbitration Service carried out a new evaluation under the existing scheme. Although the case was dismissed in the tribunal, equal value became an important criteria in the later evaluation.

The effect on women's earnings

Women's earnings relative to men's have not to date shown any significant improvement since the Equal Pay Act was amended in 1984. However, Table 6.3 does show that a small improvement in women's relative earnings has taken place.

Table 6.3   Women's earnings as a percentage of men's, 1984–7

	%
1984	73.5
1985	74.0
1986	74.3
1987	76.3

Source: New Earnings Surveys, Part A.

This is a reflection of the small number of successful equal value cases and the relatively low impact that equal value has had in collective bargaining overall. Although some women have benefited from significant improvements in relative wage rates as a result of equal value, the proportion is too small to make an overall impact on relative pay scales. This is compounded by the fact that women work fewer hours than men, and are more likely to work part-time and receive lower shift and bonus pay. It is also a reflection of the distribution of average earnings where women continue to be clustered into low-pay areas of work. For instance in 1987 46 per cent of women earned less than £110 per week compared to only 10 per cent of men.

Employers' responses to equal value

Equal value was not favourably received by employers who faced increased wage costs as a result of the amended Act. It is possible for employers to institute or modify a job evaluation scheme in order to avoid equal value claims. Such action was recommended to employers in 1982 and employers were advised to consider establishing their own evaluation schemes on a voluntary basis.

There is also evidence to suggest that employers have sought legitimate means of avoiding the terms of the equal value amendments. For instance, there has been a growth in the use of management consultants used for advice for this purpose. According to the Working Time Analysts' Report: 'that cannot by any stretch of the imagination be described as compatible with normal standards of professional conduct' (Labour Research Department, 1986).

TRADE UNIONS AND EQUAL VALUE

The trade union movement has taken the issue of equal pay as one to be achieved primarily through collective bargaining. It has been deeply suspicious of any attempts at state intervention in wage regulation. This strategy has been more successful in achieving equal pay than taking cases through the tribunals. Nevertheless, trade union support of cases in tribunals increased significantly in the 1980s and 1990s.

Where the law has been used it is clear that this has not always been with the full support of male trade unionists, who historically have held onto their privileged position in the labour market. There have been fears about the upsetting of clearly defined pay differentials and the traditional segregation of the labour market which leaves men in relatively superior positions regarding pay and other conditions.

In order to assess the impact of the EC's policy of equal value towards women on the trade union movement, a survey was conducted of 20 trade unions at the national level in 1983 and 1984. It sought to assess attitudes to the EC's policy of equal pay, and the incorporation of the principle of equal pay for work of equal value in the Equal Pay Act. The survey was unable to assess the full extent to which rank and file union members would accept equal value.

The first questionnaire was sent before the amendment to the Equal Pay Act took place. At this stage all 15 unions who responded were aware that the EC had a policy of equal pay as found in both Article 119 and the 1975 Directive. They were of the view that the EC's policy of equal pay, would be of benefit to women in trade unions.

However, many were critical of the limitations this imposed since the Government had minimised the potentially positive effect of equal pay for work of equal value. For example, the local government union, NALGO, saw that this would be of potential benefit in that it could strengthen the Act and 'thus aid collective bargaining'. This is particularly important since it is clear that collective bargaining would not automatically ensure better pay settlements for women. Legislation was seen as an important catalyst for this. The civil service union, CPSA, expressed some reservations about the legislation: 'Its effect is undoubtedly limited given employers' confidence and the lack of any real enforcement procedures'.

At one level the provisions were welcomed for their ability to set equal value on the bargaining agenda, while at another level, union hostility to legislation was reinforced, since the Government had no intention of giving realistic rights to equal value from the start.

Despite the awareness of the EC's policy at the national level, the unions who responded varied in the emphasis taken in informing women members of the policy either through publicity or in preparing for equal value claims. Several unions had taken no steps whatsoever, while others had actively sought to inform union members of developments in the EC.

Few unions had made use of or were aware of the direct effect of Article 119 and had relied principally on the Equal Pay Act when fighting for equal pay claims in the tribunals.

All unions saw that the Equal Pay Act had had little or no effect on the pay of women workers. Where it had some effect, several unions saw that it had outlived its usefulness. The Act was seen to have had limited scope, it lacked enforcement and was highly complex. Collective claims were impossible to make and the Act had largely been ineffective in bringing women up from the lowest pay scales. A few unions had recommended amendments to the Act so that the concept of equal pay for work of equal value could be realistically enforced and implemented. The concept of the notional man, or comparisons being made without a male comparator, was seen by most unions as necessary for realistic claims. Recommendations were also made to enable collective claims to take place and for removing the burden of proof from the woman onto the employer. Several unions saw the need for a looser and less rigid definition of equal work, and the need to amalgamate the provisions of the Equal Pay and Sex Discrimination Acts into one workable piece of legislation.

All unions were adamant in their total support for an effective Equal Pay Act. The issue of women's pay was seen to be particularly important in the light of the economic climate and government policies that were affecting women's security in the labour market. The family-based means of looking at women's pay was criticised, when women were increasingly having to take the role of breadwinner or of preventing the family from falling into poverty. At another level it was seen to be essential to promote women's rights at a time when women were increasingly being pushed into the home. Several unions were also clear that the amended Act, despite its complexities, was essential as a tool to fight the low pay of women workers.

The survey showed that equal pay in isolation was not one of the major legislative priorities or courses of action, but rather part of a broader strategy. For example, NALGO stressed that equal pay legislation fails to remove 'women's ghettos' and thus does little to increase women's overall pay. As a result they argued for 'positive action to break down job segregation, and action to re-evaluate women's work is therefore more important to NALGO than a simple "equal pay" approach'. Childcare and workplace nurseries featured as an important priority for many unions. Other issues such as improved maternity provision, on-the-job health checks for breast and cervical cancer, equal rights for part-time workers, shorter working hours, and positive policies to reduce job segregation were raised as part of this broader strategy.

Thirteen unions responded to follow-up questionnaires in 1984, after the Act had been amended. Unions were again assessed on their knowledge of the provisions in order to see if their understanding of them, and of the way in which they could be used, had improved. It also sought to establish the plans unions were making for tribunal applications and for collective bargaining.

A wider knowledge of the newly amended Equal Pay Act was demonstrated by most unions. Several unions had taken an active role in informing members and officials of their implications, by actively seeking cases that could be taken under the new regulations. Others had also published or were in the process of publishing union pamphlets explaining how the regulations worked. Conferences and training sessions had also been organised to help women members understand the regulations and to seek ways of using them in the tribunals. Many unions were also seeking precedents in the tribunals and the success of the case brought by Julie Hayward against Cammell Laird in the industrial tribunal was welcomed by many unions. The Banking, Finance and Insurance Union, BIFU, argued that: 'It is difficult to say how the amendments will operate – we will have to wait for precedents. Until we can see how they work out we will concentrate on pushing the equal value concept through negotiation.'

Most unions saw that the amendments would only be used in the industrial tribunals as a last resort. Rather they thought that claims would be sought initially through collective bargaining. For instance, in giving advice to union officials and shop stewards one union argued that 'the new regulations should only be employed if negotiations fail'. The Union of Construction, Allied Trades and Technicians, UCATT, similarly responded that 'legislation has to be the backdrop to workplace negotiations'. Likewise the Electrical, Electronic, Telecommunication and Plumbing Union, EETPU (1984), argued that:

> The new law on equal pay for equal value is complicated. The best way for trade unionists to use it is as a back-up, to strengthen *negotiated* claims for equal pay. However, when negotiation fails then it is important that the law is used as it is only by using it that legal decisions will be made and the principle of equal value properly established.

This attitude towards the regulations was evident from all the unions surveyed. The change in the law, to provide for equal value, was seen as a useful tool for collective bargaining strategies. The CPSA hoped that the renegotiation of the civil service pay system, to include job evaluation, would benefit women now that equal value could be negotiated using the new regulations. However, they argued that if the new system was imposed administratively 'we may well use the legislation to pursue claims'. Collective bargaining was seen to be a far more important front to improve the pay of larger numbers of women workers, whereas the legislation, in its failure to enable collective or class claims meant that 'individual claims are isolating, costly and time consuming for women. But they are of course cheaper for employers' (Pay and Benefits Bulletin, 1988). Several unions had already used the principle of equal value in negotiations and UCATT had won a pay rise by threatening tribunal action.

Most unions remained sceptical of the uses of legislation as a tool for collective bargaining and litigation in the courts as a means of achieving better pay for women workers. A wider strategy was viewed to be necessary, given the limitations of the Act. Several unions saw this wider strategy was essential to improve women's earnings, by tackling low pay across the board. Flat rate increases for women and a national minimum wage were regarded to be of greater benefit to women's earnings than equal pay legislation. The National Union of Tailors and Garment Workers, NUTGW, argued that 'a national minimum wage set at an appropriate level would have a greater impact on low pay of women clothing workers than any provisions for equal pay for work of equal value'. It saw that the principle of equal pay for work of equal value was

of some importance to women in the clothing industry. However, even if fully implemented it would not solve the problem of low pay as there is a very small proportion of male production workers, which reduces the chances of a successful comparison – and the men themselves are often also low paid.

A broader strategy, as shown from the first survey in 1983, was seen to be more appropriate than a single equal pay policy. These included some of the issues taken up by the Women's TUC, including childcare and maternity leave, genuine equal opportunities through stronger legislation, greater participation of women in unions, better education and training for women and a change to traditions and prejudices. For instance, NALGO argued that:

The value placed on women's work is not determined solely in the workplace – the relationship between home and work will have to change radically before women have true equality at work.

Despite this, most unions saw that the principle of equal pay for work of equal value would be of enormous help given the inadequacies of the

Equal Pay Act, not least in tackling 'job segregation and comparisons with manual workers' (Association of Professional, Executive, Clerical and Computer Staff (APEX)). For BIFU it was seen as:

> Very important . . . because in the banking and finance industry there are whole categories of jobs which fall outside the job evaluation schemes. . . . These are predominantly female jobs and equal value would enable us to argue that they should be compared with men's jobs.

However, the regulations were found to be complex, difficult to understand, often unworkable and full of hurdles. The NUTGW saw that:

> The complexity of the amendments to the Equal Pay Act and the procedural regulations will necessitate legal representation if women are to make successful use of them. In so far as the intention behind the establishment of industrial tribunals was to enable cases to be presented without legal representation and without undue formality, the regulations are clearly unworkable. However, they do create opportunities which did not exist before in British law.

The biggest concerns expressed were those relating to the material difference defence available to employers, the expense of taking cases to the Industrial Tribunals and the fact that the 'whole process may be too cumbersome for individual women' (Association of Scientific, Technical and Managerial Staffs).

Unions were also asked to state whether they thought there would be any problems arising for industrial relations and opposition from male members. Just over half of the unions felt that there would be some difficulties, although some were not sure to what extent this would be. BIFU anticipated 'big problems' with industrial relations and felt that male members would be opposed to equal value claims by threatening a reduction in differentials. Tess Woodcraft from NALGO also anticipated problems: 'men don't have a shining history of supporting women workers' fights for equal pay, as it is'. One union, APEX, argued that the differentials *should* be maintained and as a result saw that this would avoid difficulties in industrial relations: 'in terms of manual worker comparisons if equal pay is granted, then they could claim the better non-wage conditions of employment, a claim we would in fact support'. This was a clear indication that equal value would not be encouraged where it could lead to a widespread disruption to established differentials. The Technical, Administrative and Supervisory Section of the Engineering Workers Union (TASS) also saw problems: 'individual claims could cut across union-negotiated grading structures. Possible antagonism of male members unwilling to reconsider the value of women's work . . . a claim could involve all unions on site, therefore possible inter-union tensions'.

The CPSA also saw that 'any cases would be likely to involve inter-union opposition rather than intra-union problems'. The NUTGW did not anticipate problems from male members, but foresaw that 'there may be industrial relations implications if an employer is unhappy at being taken to an industrial tribunal by the union'. Several unions argued that there should be a wider strategy to improve the pay of all workers since a movement upwards was good for everyone.

Collective bargaining and equal value

Despite the inadequacies of the legislation, more unions were aware of the uses that can be made of equal value as a collective bargaining tool. Nevertheless, this legislation has played a vital role in supporting and buttressing women's pay claims through collective bargaining, and in altering the perception of many trade unions to the bargaining process. There is no doubt that if the legislation on equal value had not been enshrined in the law, most unions would not have taken it up in bargaining strategies. As a result an increasing number of unions have been using equal value arguments in collective bargaining.

Tribunal applications have been used as an important tactic in negotiations for revised pay structures. For example, in 1986 APEX was able to negotiate a 20 per cent pay increase for clerical workers who claimed equal value with male storekeepers at Berry Magicoal after lodging a tribunal application. Since 1984 it has become evident that more unions have backed equal value claims in attempts to regrade jobs and in negotiating criteria of equal value into job evaluation schemes.

Equal pay for work of equal value has gained greater recognition amongst unions, particularly those with large female membership. For instance, evidence given by the National Union of Public Employees to the Nursing, Staffs, Midwives and Health Visitors Review body showed the large potential that exists for nurses' pay. It showed that staff nurses could be compared with male National Health Service workers, for example electricians who earn £1000 a year more than staff nurses.

It is becoming increasingly recognised that collective bargaining is the most feasible and logical way of introducing the principle of equal value. This approach has gained wide support from the Equal Opportunities Commission and women's organisations, who recognise the difficulties in making individual claims to the tribunals. Successful case law has provided an additional lever to collective bargaining and this has established an important backdrop to union negotiations. As a result the Equal Opportunities Commission (1988a, 1988b) has directed its attention away from using the courts to encouraging a greater use of collective bargaining to end discrimination. It argues that: 'It will save employers from having to defend potentially long and costly sex discrimination and equal pay claims. And it will save women from the stress and pressures of having to take individual tribunal cases to claim their rights' (p. 1). This was backed up by a survey carried out by the Labour Research Department of 21 major unions, which showed that collective bargaining can be successfully used in removing bottom grades, in merging women's grades with men's grades, in giving flat rate increases and in targeting minimum wages (LRD, 1986).

Many unions have shown an active interest in the equal value provisions, introduced as a result of EC pressure. Despite the severe limitations of the regulations, many unions have expressed and demonstrated a commitment to using them either for equal pay claims or as a back-up to collective bargaining. There is also an awareness amongst some unions of resistance from male trade unionists, since the amended Act now enables broader comparisons to be made. This has the potential of upsetting historical and prejudicial differentials between women's and men's wages.

The attitude of all unions to the amended legislation has been equivocal, in that it has failed to alter significantly women's earnings and more importantly to tackle low pay and job segregation. For instance NALGO (1983):

considers the question of equal pay for work of equal value to be of central importance to women workers. That women's pay is often low pay is axiomatic and women's low pay is clearly associated with the low value placed on their skills and responsibilities. (p. 3)

CONCLUSION

This chapter has shown the way in which the European Court's ruling was interpreted by the Government and the procedure and consultations that took place to implement the principle into policy. The UK Government's reluctance to introduce the principle of equal value in a positive way was modified by interest group participation in this process. Despite this the 1984 amendment has been heavily criticised for its complexities. The EC Commission has been unable to influence this process, despite its criticisms of the Government's attempts to abide by EC law. The Equal Opportunities Commission (1983) was clear that 'The adoption of the amendments as they stand may well lead to further, protracted, complex and costly litigation to establish individual claims in domestic and, eventually, European Courts' (p. 4). As a result the Equal Opportunities Commission has recommended that the legislation be amended to bring it in line with EC standards. Its proposals have sought to consolidate the Equal Pay and Sex Discrimination Act and to incorporate the relevant requirements of EC law directly into national legislation (EOC, 1986, 1989).

This chapter has also looked at the effect of the amended Equal Pay Act and its implementation in practice. Equal value has had some effect on women's relative pay rates, but its use in the tribunals has been limited. Since claims are made by individuals, employers are under no obligation to regrade and revalue the work of all women. Collective bargaining, on the other hand, is seen as one area where a real impact on women's pay can be achieved. Many unions have actively used the equal value regulations and have sought strategic ways of implementing them into collective bargaining. In addition, it is clear that equal value has regenerated the issue of equal pay in collective bargaining. It has brought new strategies onto the bargaining table that would not have been possible without the influence of EC policy.

This case study of the implementation of the equal pay directive in the UK provides an understanding of the complex relationship between the EC and member states. Of particular importance is the way in which a member state can affect the implementation of a directive in a manner that seeks to restrict its practical impact. This has implications for the implementation of all aspects of EC policy. Indeed this became even more crucial in the run-up to the single market as the need to introduce policies to protect women from the effects of new forms of competition placed a higher priority on the development of policy for women. The next chapter looks at the policies that have been developed for women in the single market.

7 Policies for Women in the Single European Market, 1986–92

INTRODUCTION

The passing of the Single European Act in 1986 brought a new wave of interest to the EC's social dimension. It released the EC from its deadlock in policy-making, in both the economic and social fields. It injected a new political will into a community burdened with indecision and lack of direction and defined the role of the EC for the 1990s and beyond. In some senses the creation of a single market was a necessary response to the growing internationalisation of trade and competition. However, an unequal Community cannot be a real Community unless strong social measures are developed to protect women from competition and from new forms of exploitation.

The Single European Act's 280 legislative proposals aim to create an internal market with no barriers to the movement of capital, goods, services and labour. Although the Act makes reference to the need for the single market to promote both economic and social cohesion, it does not define clearly what it means by this other than the reduction of regional inequalities through a reform and strengthening of the European Social Fund and the Regional Development Fund.

Of particular importance has been the shift away from unanimous voting to majority voting in the Council of Ministers. However, social and labour policies, excluding health and safety at work, remain subject to unanimous voting in the Council of Ministers. There is scope for introducing the bulk of policies relating to the social dimension through majority voting if it can be broadly determined that they are related to health and safety at work, or that social issues could undermine the Single European Act due to the distortion of competition.[1] In addition a new system of legislative cooperation was introduced in the Act. This gave the European Parliament and the Commission greater influence in determining new policies and suggesting amendments to the Council of Ministers.[2]

This stage saw a growing commitment in the EC to the social dimension, if only as a bulwark to unfettered economic activity. Women also became increasingly vocal. The formation of the

European Women's Lobby, more networking between women's groups, trade unions and interest groups, the continuing pressure from the European Parliament Women's Committee and the Commission's Equal Opportunities Unit, gave women's interests a much more visible focus than had existed hitherto. However, the stage was met with considerable opposition from the UK, with several member states hiding behind its position, on the implementation of the Social Charter on Workers' Rights.

In the social field it became increasingly necessary to ensure that closer cooperation in Europe did not lead to any one group or individual being disadvantaged. Considerable pressure was put on the EC by the European Trade Union Confederation (ETUC) and the European Parliament to develop a set of social rights. The ETUC (1988) argued that there was a need for social policies to guarantee minimum standards in pay, working conditions, social security, equal opportunities, health and safety, and workers' consultation 'if the internal market is to be completed in a dynamic and equitable manner' (p. 3). For the women's policy it opened up a whole new debate about the impact of the single market on women's employment and the need for policies to counteract the disadvantages women face. In the development of further policies for women the debate about the 'social dimension' stressed the need for a stronger and more effective social policy to ensure that all citizens of Europe were able to benefit from integration in the economic and social spheres. Chapters 2 and 3 showed that women start from a weaker position than men in competing for jobs in the single market, and more crucially that the positive benefits of the single market would not automatically or necessarily extend to women. In this respect both the European Parliament and Commission, and a growing lobby of women, have injected a more forceful argument into this debate. They have argued that without a stronger EC women's policy, women will lose out significantly in the completion and operation of the internal market.

DEVELOPING POLICIES FOR WOMEN IN THE SINGLE EUROPEAN MARKET

The Social Charter

As the programme to complete the internal market got under way it became increasingly clear that an economic market also necessitated a 'social dimension' as the social costs of the single market would not necessarily benefit all regions of the EC and all groups in the population. Thus, warnings by the Commission and the European Parliament that the single market could create new patterns of inequality and social exclusion and that the single market would affect women in a different way to men was followed up by a series of social policies designed to protect women in Europe from some of the rigours of the single market. The Social Charter on Workers' Rights was widely welcomed by trade unions and women throughout the Community and by 11 of the 12 member states (Commission of the ECs, 1990c). It stated that in the context of the single European market 'the same importance must be attached to the social aspects as to the economic aspects'. However, this was principally designed to ensure the economic competitiveness of the regions and employment development and creation.

Issues relating to a guaranteed minimum income for all people, whether in work or not, training, the right to free movement of labour, rights of trade unions and women, were formulated into a draft Social Charter. However, it was substantially watered down before it was agreed at the Strasbourg Summit in December 1989, where the UK Government voiced its total opposition. The decision to go ahead without the UK's agreement resulted from the frustration of the other member states to the UK's obstructive role in this area and in this sense the UK was isolated in its criticisms. The UK was not only opposed to most of the provisions of the Charter, but also to its very substance. It viewed the Charter as being beyond the responsibilities of the EC and considered that the effect of the Charter would be to risk jobs and create further unemployment. This was despite the fact that many of the proposals outlined in the Charter were accepted as standard practice in other member states whose employment rates had, in any event, grown at a faster rate than in the UK. The text of the finally agreed Charter can be found in Appendix 6.

For instance, the proposals for a 'decent wage' were already established practice in several member states. France, Spain, The Netherlands, Portugal and Luxembourg have existing state-regulated minimum wages and in Greece and Belgium these were fixed between employers and unions at a national level. In Italy, Germany and Denmark collective agreements set minimum levels of pay and these were extended to workers not covered by agreements in Italy and Germany, whereas in Denmark 90 per cent of workers were covered by minimum wages through collective agreements. Although in Ireland and the UK it is possible to set minimum wages, wages councils in the UK have been eroded and face abolition, while in Ireland the coverage has been extended to more workers.

In other key controversial areas of the Charter relating to working conditions, the rights of trade unions and workers' rights to consultation and information, the UK similarly fell behind the legal protection and rights established in other EC states. In many senses the proposals in the Social Charter go against the grain of the UK's thinking on the regulation of pay and trade union rights. It had not spent over ten years deregulating the labour market to have this imposed at a European level. It was only in relation to the proposals on free movement of labour and health, and safety at work, that there was a measure of agreement for EC action.

In relation to rights for the elderly, young people and children and people with disabilities, the Government was of a view that the EC was meddling in affairs that were not its responsibility. It did not agree with the proposals for an EC-wide system that provided the right to training for all workers through their working lives.

The finally agreed Charter represented a considerable dilution of the original draft. Its reference to 'workers' rather than 'citizens' led to the exclusion of the non-working population (the elderly, sick and disabled and unemployed) from coverage in the Charter. Likewise, many of the provisions that had originally placed a responsibility on the EC to develop policies were left in the hands of member states. This covered, for instance, areas relating to the right to strike, the rights of legally resident migrant workers, the right to training, the development of childcare facilities and the right to a minimum standard of living and social protection.

The Charter has a specific section relating to equal treatment and equal opportunities for men and women:

> To this end, action should be intensified to ensure the implementation of the principle of equality between men and women as regards in particular access to employment, remuneration, working conditions, social protection, education, vocational training and career development.

It calls for measures to enable men and women to reconcile occupational and family responsibilities and is limited in its reference to women in paid work.

The Social Charter treats women as a homogeneous group and fails to discuss the specific effects of discrimination and prejudice on particular groups of women. For instance, no attempt was made to address the specific needs of disabled women, of black and ethnic minority women and lesbians. Nor did it attempt to deal with the very particular forms of discrimination that these groups face. Other sections of the Charter dealing with elderly people and disabled people similarly did not address the specific disadvantages and problems faced by older women and disabled women. The European Parliament was unsuccessful in prompting the EC to introduce equal retirement age and equality in pensions as well as the right to home care into the Social Charter.

In other respects the Social Charter is unclear and fails to give clear meaning to its definition of 'family' in both the section on equal treatment between men and women and the section on free movement of labour. Could this also mean lesbian or gay families? In Denmark and France, where it is illegal to discriminate against lesbians and gay men, it could well be interpreted widely, whereas the UK, which has the most punitive and restrictive laws on homosexuality in the EC, would resist a more liberal definition of the family.

Nevertheless, the Social Charter's silence on lesbian and gay rights has been cause for concern across Europe, particularly in relation to free movement of labour. It has been estimated that out of Europe's population of 820 million people, between 50 and 60 million people are lesbian or gay. The absence of any protection against discrimination is particularly important in the single market as lesbians or gay men seek to move from one country to another only to find different laws and rights than their country of origin. For instance, the more liberal laws in Denmark that permit and recognise gay marriages would be of no use to a Danish gay couple seeking to move to other EC countries with more restricted laws. As a result there have been calls from the gay movement across Europe to develop common EC policies on lesbian and gay rights, based on the more liberal laws found in Denmark and The Netherlands (Tatchell, 1990).

Lesbian and gay rights have prompted some attention in the Parliament and Commission. In 1984 the European Parliament accepted the need for equal rights for lesbian and gay men when it adopted the report drawn up by Italian Communist, Vera Squarcialupi MEP (Squarcialupi, 1983). However, the EC did not take up the issue. The Social Charter did provide another good opportunity to raise the question of lesbian and gay rights. A report drawn up by French socialist, Martine Buron MEP, calling for the Social Charter to ensure that all workers receive protection regardless of sexual preference, also failed to push the EC into action (Buron, 1989). In 1991 the EC Commission for the first time considered the possibility of looking into the issue of lesbian and gay rights, but was clear that it was not within the scope of the Treaties for the EC to feel obliged to address the issue.

Likewise the right to equal treatment irrespective of race, colour and religion was not guaranteed in the Social Charter. The response of the EC to developing rights for black and ethnic minority people has been dismal compared to the policies developed for women. In one sense this reflects the very low priority given to the rights of the non-voting 'migrants' of Europe, who have little visibility or political power (the EC treaties only refer to citizens, not to residents). The Social Charter made no specific mention of racism or racial discrimination, although the Council of Ministers was forced to include a broad statement in the preamble to the Charter after protest from migrant and refugee groups in Europe:

> in order to ensure equal treatment it is important to combat every form of discrimination, including discrimination on grounds of sex, colour, race, opinions and beliefs, and whereas, in a spirit of solidarity, it is important to combat social exclusion;

It went on to argue that legally resident workers from non-EC countries and their families 'are able to enjoy, as regards their living and working conditions, treatment comparable to that enjoyed by workers who are nationals of the member state concerned'. However, this was not backed up by legislative proposals and it remains a statement of intent. This is particularly important since many migrant workers are excluded from the Charter's provisions. Black, refugee and migrant groups across Europe are becoming increasingly vocal in their demands for the recognition of the important and vital contribution they make to European prosperity. However, the EC has failed to respond to their demands in policy. The proposals from the European Parliament's Committee of Inquiry into Racism and Xenophobia in Europe, for a Charter for migrant workers, have nevertheless fuelled the debate about the need for greater protection for migrant workers (European Parliament, 1990b).

Action Programme from the Social Charter

In order to implement the Social Charter the Commission drew up an Action Programme containing 47 proposals for legislative action (Commission of the ECs, 1989e). It did, however, recognise that 'the harmonization of systems is illusory, given their diversity and history'.

Of particular interest is that many of the proposals for directives were able to be decided on the basis of majority voting in the Council, preventing one member state from implementing a veto. Although the Action Programme contained a number of important measures of direct relevance to women, it did not go as far as many women's groups had expected. The Action Programme represented a further watering-down of the Social Charter and included many proposals of a non-binding nature. Tom Megahy, MEP, argued that: 'The declared aim of ensuring that working men and women share in the benefits of the single market or are protected from the difficulties it will bring has been forgotten. Market forces are to be allowed to drive down wages and undermine working conditions' (undated, p. 1).

Progress in implementing the Social Charter through the Social Action Programme has been very slow. Although proposals for directives and other legislative acts had were made during 1990 and 1991 their adoption was hampered by indecision about majority voting and the failure of several member states, most notably the UK, to agree in principle to their terms.

The proposals in the Action Programme on women's rights included a third Community action programme on equal opportunities for women, directives on the protection of pregnant women at work and on atypical work, recommendations on childcare and a code of conduct on the protection of pregnancy and maternity. In addition the Commission saw the need to 'examine what legal and positive action measures are necessary to ensure that the rights enshrined in Community law on the principle of equality are fully available in practice at the national level'.

The Commission also put pressure on the Council of Ministers to continue its discussions on the three draft directives on parental leave, on the reversal of the burden of proof and on retirement age. Despite considerable pressure no proposals were made on discrimination on the grounds of race, colour or religion. It left the responsibility on governments and the two sides of industry to attempt to eradicate racial discrimination in the workplace and in access to work. The Action Programme also proposed a third action programme for people with disabilities (1992–6) and a directive covering travel conditions for disabled workers. However, the EC did not go as far as addressing the issue of discrimination against people with disabilities nor did it address the specific disadvantages that disabled women face both in the workplace and in society at large.

In September 1990 the European Parliament passed a resolution based on a report of the Social Affairs Committee. While welcoming the Action Programme, it was critical of the lack of legal weight attached to some of the proposals and the absence of measures in a number of key areas. On women, the Parliament made a number of recommendations that went beyond the scope of the Action Programme and were related to ensuring minimum levels of protection to prevent women falling into poverty and programmes to help the integration of women into the labour market. It argued that:

> the potential advantages of the single market cannot be produced automatically and therefore a good social policy must be an integral part of Community policy, since there is a real danger that greater competitiveness will be achieved at the price of a deterioration in living conditions for women . . . social marginalisation and exclusion are totally unacceptable in the European Community, in which social and economic progress must go hand in hand. (European Parliament, 1990a, p. 6)

As well as calling for a legal framework for member states' compliance with the directives, the Parliament recommended the introduction of a legal definition of equal value and indirect discrimination, and the implementation of outstanding directives. It went on to argue that equal treatment should be applied to the drawing up of job classification schemes and these, along with statutory minimum wages, should be reviewed to take account of the value of women's work. Trade unions were seen to play a vital role in negotiating against direct and indirect discrimination. It also called on stronger provisions in the area of vocational training, that ensured that half of the beneficiaries of the European Social Fund were women and that 'assistance from the ESF and the ERDF be made dependent on the availability of childcare in employment and training situations and in compliance with the directives on equal treatment' (European Parliament, 1990a, p. 17). In addition, it called for directives covering childcare, positive action, sexual harassment and the protection of pregnant women, along with measures to combat poverty amongst women.

Third Action Programme on equal opportunities

The third Community programme on equal opportunities was informally agreed in April 1989 by ministers responsible for women's affairs. With the second programme on equal opportunities ending in 1990, it was recognised that a new programme was needed to tackle the specific issues facing women with the completion of the internal market. The Action Programme introduced in January 1991 aimed to provide measures to ensure that women are not left in a disadvantaged position in the single market through four areas for action.

First, it placed a much greater emphasis on the 'social dialogue' between employers and unions, something to which the Community is generally giving a high profile in the internal market. It argued that equal opportunities should be placed much higher on the agenda of trade unions and employers' organisations. With this in mind there was a feeling that the 'social partners' should take a much greater role with member states in implementing the Action Programme. Second, higher priority was given to childcare and combining family and occupational responsibilities. Third, a new emphasis was given to the role of women in decision-making in public authorities, advisory and consultative bodies and councils that advise governments. This led to the setting up of a new network to advise the Commission on how to promote women in decision-making bodies. Fourth, more emphasis was given to the integration of women into the mainstream of the economy and social life to enable women to gain access to more power and higher positions in work and decision-making.

As with the previous action programmes on equal opportunities, these were statements of intent, to be backed up with further legislative action. They included a number of legislative proposals that will now be discussed.

Pregnancy at work

The proposed directive on the protection of pregnant women at work was the result of a long-standing concern about the health and safety of women at work, that frequently failed to address the particular effects that the working environment had on pregnant women. However, its final form was a compromise. Women's organisations and trade unions had called for a wider-ranging directive that covered pregnancy and maternity rights for all women. The Commission was of the view that such a proposal would not get past the Council of Ministers. Instead a proposal that fell more neatly into the Commission's programme of preparing employment protection and rights in the context of the internal market was chosen. In many senses the Commission viewed that this would be the first step in alerting the Council to the need for EC action for pregnant women and to give protection initially to those women who were most at risk in the workplace.

The aim of the directive is to set a minimum EC standard and to overcome the barriers pregnant women face in employment. It covers women in all forms of employment, whether standard or atypical, regardless of whether they receive maternity rights or not at the national level. The proposals include protection for pregnant or breast-feeding women from working conditions and working hours that are detrimental to their health and security, but without a loss of their employment rights or pay. As part of the Commission's health and safety in the workplace 'clean-up' it also protects pregnant or breast-feeding women from exposure to physical, biological or chemical agents and processes. Trade unions had argued that the directive should have gone further by protecting the reproductive rights of men and women from genetic damage from chemical substances and processes, along the lines of the developments taking place in the USA.

The directive also proposed that maternity leave is a right for working women or women who had been registered unemployed since the beginning of their pregnancy. This would give women the right to 14 weeks' leave with an allowance and/or the same pay they received in work. Pregnant women would also benefit from compulsory leave of at least two weeks, before the birth of the child.

Of particular significance is that this directive is proposed to take effect under majority voting in the Council. The UK opposed the directive and argued that it would create unnecessary rigidities in the labour market, leading to higher labour costs and less employment for women. In the UK about 60 per cent of working women have no rights to maternity leave. This is largely because women have to have worked for the same employer full-time for two years or part-time for five years. This restrictive provision fails to recognise the inflexible and atypical forms of work that women are engaged in. Given that women in the UK have some of the lowest entitlements to protection at work and maternity leave, the UK's line has been defensive to say the least. The draft directive was formally agreed by the Council of Ministers in November 1991, after several revisions insisted on by the UK government. Its final form does little to extend women's maternity rights in the UK, but it does prevent other member states from 'levelling down' to the UK's already low levels of provision.

Pregnancy and maternity

In the protection of pregnancy and maternity the issue of subsidiarity was raised. It was recognised that in this area social protection should be a national objective, and that the EC could only intervene where necessary to establish minimum rules. As a result a recommendation was proposed giving a code of good conduct in protection for pregnancy and maternity.

Childcare

The proposal for a recommendation on good practice in childcare was a big disappointment for many women in the EC, who had been arguing for many years that a directive was necessary to establish EC-wide action on childcare. The 1989 report of the EC Childcare Network forcefully argued that a directive was vital if women were to gain equal opportunities at work and that this:

> should require Member States to develop publicly-funded childcare services for children at least up to the age of 10, with an ultimate objective of ensuring the availability of publicly-funded services for all parents who are employed or training, either free at the time of use or at a reasonable price that all parents can afford, taking into account their income and other needs. (Commission of the EC, 1989d, p. 92)

In the event, the Commission saw a recommendation as the only course of action. It was clear that a directive would not be passed by the Council of Ministers and that it was more realistic to get a non-binding initiative passed in order to set the scene for binding proposals at a later stage. The Commission was particularly cautious in its approach to this issue, but was of the opinion that suggesting a directive could set the initiative back years (interview, Pauline Conroy-Jackson, Brussels, 1990). Indeed this was the lesson that had been learnt from the proposed directives on part-time work and temporary work in 1983–4, which had taken seven years to get back onto the agenda again.

On the question of EC competence, the childcare issue has been particularly controversial and often confused. The question of subsidiarity has arisen in the actual provision of childcare for the under-fives, since this has been restrictively viewed as an educational responsibility by member states. Since the Treaty of Rome does not give the EC responsibility in education, this has been used as an excuse to apply subsidiarity to childcare. However, it is widely recognised that childcare is vital if women are to combine their family and work responsibilities and as such is an equal opportunities issue. This is evident from the important work carried out by the Childcare Network and consistent pressure from the European Parliament Women's Committee. In this area the EC has been able to establish limited competence, for instance through the New Opportunities for Women programme (see below). This has enabled the funding of pilot projects for work oriented childcare.

Since the single market requires more women to work and to be mobile, childcare is a major issue in the internal market. Indeed many of the initiatives under discussion have been directly influenced by the debate about the regional concentrations of employment growth. Since there will be shortages of skilled workers in some regions that can only be filled by women, childcare will be vital for women's access to new occupations. For instance, the shortage of skilled workers in financial services, evident in Luxembourg, has shown the need for childcare to match the supply and demand for new skilled labour.

Women, training and employment creation

The Social Charter provides the right to vocational training: 'each worker should have access to training or retraining on a conditions basis so as to minimise the adverse social impact of industrial restructuring and technological change'. Women's access to training is not specifically mentioned. Demographic changes, coupled with the steadily rising participation of women in the labour market, and growing long-term unemployment amongst women, means that women's training needs cannot be ignored. Moreover, women have lower levels of training and qualifications compared to men and have represented a smaller proportion of beneficiaries of the European Social Fund than men. Their access to training is closely tied up with the social infrastructure, including childcare, school hours, care for the elderly and so on.

In recognition of the special needs women have for training and to prevent them being marginalised in the single market, a New Opportunities for Women (NOW) programme was launched by Vasso Papendreou, in July 1990 (Commission of the EC, 1990d). It is funded through the European Social Fund (95 per cent) and the Regional Development Fund (5 per cent). It is one of three initiatives on human resource development in the context of the internal market. The NOW scheme gave a budget of 120 million ecus for three years for new initiatives in women's training and the development of small businesses and co-operatives by women (1990–3). It also included the provision of pilot projects on the funding of childcare schemes to facilitate women's re-entry into the labour market. This provides childcare for women entering training projects, childcare provision in workplaces, in industrial zones or on estates, and the means for improving the qualifications for childcare workers.

The Women's Local Employment Initiative, introduced in 1984, provides start-up grants and technical assistance for women wanting to set up small businesses and is geared to moving women out of long-term unemployment into employment creation. This is an important scheme given the trend in women's small business creation and the lack of support given to women for this. In 1989 funding was given to 212 women's businesses and in 1990 the budgetary allocation was increased to one million ecus. It prioritises women in the poorer regions of the Community and women who are unemployed, single parents, disabled women and ethnic minority women. However, the level of funding is very small and is likely to have a limited impact on the very real problems facing women in some of the peripheral regions of the Community. Nevertheless, it does prioritise women's enterprise in a way that has not been achieved at the national level and provides women with opportunities that would otherwise not have existed.

Draft directives on atypical work

In June 1990 three new draft directives on part-time and temporary work were published by the Commission, the first to be issued under the Community's Action Programme. It is estimated that there are 14 million part-time workers and 10 million temporary workers in the EC and women make up a large proportion of these. In addition women are more likely to take seasonal, casual and irregular work with varying forms of fixed duration contracts. Chapter 5 discussed the previous directives on part-time work and temporary work that were blocked by the Council of Ministers in the 1980s. The three directives proposed in 1990 replace the two old ones as well as introducing new provisions on atypical work.

The directives deal with the various problems that arise in atypical work and cover health and safety, the regulation of the spread of part-time and temporary work, and the fixing of minimum standards and conditions. They aim to give them the same *pro rata* benefits and rights as full-time and permanent workers. As with the previous directives that reached stalemate in the 1980s, renewed controversy erupted. The draft directives were forcefully opposed by the UK and Germany. Michael Howard, the UK Secretary of State for Employment in the UK, argued that the directives make it hard for companies to compete and that this would lead to job losses. In particular he argued that women and disabled people would face reduced opportunities to work part-time.

Particularly controversial is the directive on 'atypical work' which would give people working on part-time and other atypical contracts of more than eight hours a week the right to the same *pro rata* social security, holidays, redundancy pay and seniority allowances as full-time workers. Of significance is that the directive is to be subjected to majority voting in the Council of Ministers since the Commission has argued that different contracts and conditions of employment in different member states distort competition. According to the Commission this directive is vital to ensure that the growth of part-time work throughout the EC does not become a reason for reduced labour costs and 'social dumping'. This will affect the UK and Germany where 2.5 million and just under half a million part-time workers respectively, receive no social security benefits.

The second draft directive gives part-time and temporary workers the right to similar conditions of work, including training, benefits in cash and kind and social services, as full-time workers. The directive also provides that where an employer wants to use part-time and temporary workers this should be decided with workers' representatives and that part-time and temporary workers should be informed of full-time vacancies.

The third draft directive proposes that temporary workers should be covered by the same provisions of health and safety at work as other employees, should be informed of the risks they face and be entitled to training if necessary.

If the directives are adopted, they would have to be implemented by 31 December 1992. Their passage will be considerably smoother than that of their predecessors in the 1980s since opposition to them can be bypassed by majority voting in the Council of Ministers and through the greater powers conferred on the European Parliament. It is their implementation in practice that is likely to be the stumbling block for those countries reluctant to see such provisions introduced at the national level.

The directives on atypical work, the NOW programme and the third Action Programme have all been prompted by the growing concerns in the Community that women could lose out on some of the benefits that are likely to flow from the single market. This is particularly in relation to training and access to the labour market. The Commission's Equal Opportunities Unit has been particularly concerned that women face enormous disadvantages and that unequal opportunities could widen rather than narrow as competition becomes more intense. Other initiatives have not directly resulted from the internal market, but have been on the agenda for a long time.

Reversing the burden of proof

In May 1988 a draft directive was presented to the Council of Ministers on reversing the burden of proof from the claimant to the employer in equality cases. Experience of equality cases in member states had found that women were disadvantaged because they were unable to provide a sufficient level of proof of discrimination, particularly where this was indirect. As a result many cases had been unnecessarily lost because the burden of proof rested on the woman. This was recognised in the 1988 report of the 1982–5 Action Programme on women, where it was recommended that the burden of proof should be shifted to the employer, since the relevant information was usually in the hands of the employer in any case. The proposal for a directive had full support from the European Parliament, the Economic and Social Committee and the Advisory Group on Equal Opportunities. However, the directive suffered the same fate as many previous directives, being blocked by the UK in the Council of Ministers.

Despite this, a ruling by the European Court of Justice in the Danish *Danfoss* case found that where a woman was discriminated against in pay regarding additional payments given to workers based on 'flexibility', the burden of proof should shift to the employer. This had the effect of reinterpreting Article 6 of the Equal Treatment Directive which states that:

Member states shall introduce into their national systems such measures as are necessary to enable all persons who consider themselves wronged by failure to apply to them the principle of equal treatment . . . to pursue their claims by judicial process after possible recourse to other competent authorities.

As a result the EC is now in a position to require member states to comply with the reinterpretation of Article 6, thus fulfilling the aims of the blocked directive.

Retirement age

In 1989 the Commission proposed a directive on equal retirement ages, equal treatment for survivors and the ending of discrimination against women whose employment had been interrupted to bring up children. This directive was also blocked in the Council of Ministers by the UK.

Since the directive was blocked there has been an important ruling on pensions in the European Court of Justice. The 'historic' Barber ruling on occupational pensions has had the effect of widening the scope of Article 119. The court found that Article 119 covered pensions paid under contracted-out occupational pension schemes. The setting of different pensionable ages and benefits was found to be one aspect of sex discrimination. As a result this judgment has implications for discriminatory *ex gratia* payments in addition to pensions, for example in state redundancy schemes. More importantly it raises problems for the maintenance of unequal retirement ages in the EC.

Sexual harassment and violence against women

In May 1990 the Council of Ministers passed a resolution on the protection of the dignity of women and men at work. Indeed this initiative demonstrates the ability of the EC to go beyond the strict remit of the single market, where there is a will to do so. It has the potential for widening the scope of the concept of equal treatment and represents the first EC-wide definition of sexual harassment that includes 'conduct of a sexual nature, or other conduct based on sex affecting the dignity of women and men at work'. This could also potentially cover harassment of lesbians and gay men. The resolution was based on a report for the Commission by Michael Rubenstein, *Dignity at Work*, in 1989. It highlighted the effects that sexual harassment can have on working women's rights and their integration into the labour market and called for EC policy designed to include sexual harassment as an aspect of sex discrimination. This view had been expressed by the Advisory Committee on Equal Opportunities in June 1988, where a recommendation and code of conduct were proposed on sexual harassment. The European Parliament had also passed a resolution in June 1986 on violence against women and called on governments, trade unions and equal opportunities commissions/committees to develop law on sexual harassment and to inform women of their rights. The 1990 Council Resolution calls on member states to 'remind employers that they have a responsibility to seek to ensure that the work environment is free from . . . unwanted conduct of a sexual nature or other conduct based on sex affecting the dignity of women and men at work'.

National governments are asked to inform and promote awareness that sexual harassment is an aspect of sex discrimination, and to encourage both sides of industry collectively to agree policies to free the workplace of sexual harassment. The Commission was also asked to draw up a code of conduct on sexual harassment by July 1991.

Although a resolution is not binding, it is evident, following a judgment in the European Court of Justice in 1989, that the sexual harassment resolution could have more weight than anticipated (Equal Opportunities Review, 1990). Thus it could be possible for its terms to be seen within the context of the 1976 directive on equal treatment, and the resolution makes it clear that national courts and tribunals should be aware of the fact that its terms could be contrary to the principle of equal treatment in the directive.

Women and development

A resolution was passed by the Council on the role of women in the development process. It recommended a greater role for the integration of women in development and the provision of better aid to women, especially in the Lomé countries. Although going beyond the direct remit of the single market, this initiative was influenced by a growing global women's lobby and has led to the setting up of a women and development office in the Commission.

In many senses it is this mainstreaming into other areas of Commission activity that the Equal Opportunities Unit has encouraged. In addition to the women and development office and the women's information service, there now exists a women's officer in the statistical office of the EC, a women's officer for the FAST programme and a woman responsible for the NOW programme.

The development of policies for women has met with resistance from the UK, which has a long history of blocking directives that would have led to positive gains for women in the EC. This was most notable in the UK's opposition to the Social Charter.

However, the European Court of Justice has offered renewed hope for many women. Positive judgments have been given in several cases that have had the effect of extending the scope of EC law. This was evident in the cases relating to the burden of proof, sexual harassment and pensions, discussed above.

EUROPE OF THE REGIONS: CRISIS OR OPPORTUNITY?

The programme for introducing the internal market brought with it a new debate about the internal cohesion of the Community and the need to reduce internal barriers. To some extent the Single European Act gave regions a higher profile on the understanding that the internal market could not work effectively with vast regional imbalances. On the one hand, European integration could lead to the development of a new equality between the regions. It could inject a new awareness of the vast inequalities in living standards and opportunities throughout the EC, particularly as these affect women. On the other hand, it could further reinforce regional concentrations of power and employment and the decline of the least prosperous regions.

The commitment, in the 1986 Single European Act, to doubling the structural funds was one step in the direction of addressing regional inequalities. In 1989 a new system of financial support for disadvantaged regions of the Community was implemented. Between 1989 and 1993 50 billion ecus were earmarked for the structural funds. This is geared to overcoming the structural disadvantages which prevent certain regions being competitive. Priority is given to the poorest regions of the Community, including Greece, Portugal, Ireland, Northern Ireland, parts of Spain and Italy, Corsica and the French Overseas Departments. Support is also given to declining industrial and rural areas. In addition three billion ecus have been given in structural aid to East Germany to assist its integration into Europe. Aid through the structural funds continues to require the matching of funds at the national, regional or local level. However, the operation of this system has led, in some member states, to problems of distribution, equity and implementation. It has often failed to target women's specific needs and has left women on the sidelines of this regional development process.

The Commission is well aware that regional development cannot be achieved through short-term financial incentives. If regions are to be competitive there is a need for skilled workers and for infrastructure in the regions to attract business investment away from the Euro-centre. The pull to the centre is assisted by large metropolitan centres with good infrastructure, skilled workers and consumer markets. Regional development is vital to ensure that the poorer and peripheral regions are not squeezed out of this development. Skilled workers and good transport communications are of particular importance. The discussion in Chapter 3 showed that women are particularly disadvantaged in the regions where they are least likely to have access to training and skilled work.

The EC has made it illegal for state aids to secure competitive advantage. As a result EC structural support for training, research and development, telecommunications, services, and so on, will be crucial to ensure equal competition between regions. This will increasingly have to tackle training and education as priorities on a larger scale and to involve women at the centre of plans for development. But how far will this structural support convince firms to move out of the Euro-centre into the peripheral regions?

The decline in agriculture will see further migration to the big cities. Likewise shortages of labour in some of the big cities could lead to higher levels of immigration from North Africa and East Europe to the large centres. As a result of discussions in EFTA and the EC the accession of new EC members is likely. By 1991 five countries (Austria, Cyprus, Malta, Sweden and Turkey) had applied for membership of the EC, at a time when other members of EFTA, and several central and eastern European countries were also considering applications and where association agreements were also being negotiated with Czechoslovakia, Hungry and Poland. By 1996 the EC could be made up of as many as 20 member states. This could inject a new pressure and commitment to women's policies from the countries with a long-standing commitment to social policies and the rights of women. New trade and economic cooperation with Eastern European countries could see further applications, in the long term, for membership from these economically weaker countries. There is also the possibility of increased access to Eastern European markets and the potential for low cost manufacturing in these areas in the long term. Could these trends lead to even greater concentrations in the core areas of development and further exacerbate existing regional inequalities?

The movement to full Economic and Monetary Union (EMU) places more pressure on the need for stronger countervailing measures for the peripheral and poorer regions. The Commission sees the benefits of a single currency for higher growth and convergence in the Community. However, convergence is not an automatic by-product of EMU. Indeed the risk of greater inequality in living standards is high. EMU requires convergence from the start. Budget deficits and high interest rates place some countries at an immediate disadvantage compared to the 'healthier' economies in Europe. This requires an even larger role for structural support in the short and long term. The Commission has proposed a new scheme of financial support to assist with the economic problems arising from EMU for some of the poorer member states and regions. This has led to demands that more political responsibility and accountability needs to be given to the regions to redress the concentrations of power and decision-making at the European level. Decentralising powers to the regions and the setting up of stronger regional bodies could help to redress the centralisation of decision-making. Full regional involvement in decision-making is vital to ensure regional involvement in planning and policy making. Indeed, the regions are best placed to implement their own development and to represent their own interests at the Community level.

The December 1991 Maastricht summit agreed in principle to set up a regional consultative committee made up of representatives from member states' regional and local authorities. This would act as a consultative body, with advisory status, alongside the European Parliament and the Economic and Social Committee. Of its 189 seats, 24 would be given to each of the larger member states, Germany, France, Italy and the UK. The regional committee is particularly favoured by Germany, whose regional bodies already enjoy decision-making, legislative and financial powers at the regional level.

Women could benefit from such a structure, but only if their specific needs and interests were represented at a political level. There is no automatic guarantee of this, given women's under-representation at all political and decision-making levels, despite it being marginally better at the local or regional level. However, there would be more scope for women's representation at the regional level, particularly since women are more likely to be affected by shifts in mobility than men. However, there is more likelihood that women will be well placed to network and develop strategies at the local or regional level, than exists at the national or European level. Indeed it is at these levels that women are beginning to network and organise, and they too are keen to be at the centre of regional development and decision-making.

Moreover, the competitive capacity of many regions, coupled with demographic trends, has placed a high profile on women's contribution to regional prosperity. The Commission has not recognised the particular barriers regions may face in the development of infrastructure to assist women's competitive positions. For instance, while the Regional Development Fund gives assistance for infrastructure, it fails to recognise that childcare is one aspect of this.

Issues relating to training and retraining, and social infrastructure, including childcare, are political issues that regions must take seriously in decision-making. Commission studies and reports have failed to address the specific problems women face in regional development. Within the regions themselves, inadequate networks have prevented the representation of women's interests, although these are gaining a higher profile.

Debates about national sovereignty have failed to recognise the possibilities of achieving greater sovereignty at a regional level since they are tied up with new forms of sovereignty at the European level. It is no longer appropriate to discuss national sovereignty in the context of the international economy, where national economic decisions are closely tied up with international decisions. If this exists at the economic level, then what place or role is left for national political sovereignty? In the UK this has been used to justify opposition to policies that are viewed to be politically or ideologically in conflict with national political priorities. Economic and monetary union has moved at a much faster pace than political union. Indeed the UK Government has accepted the swift development of economic union, whilst resisting political union. This has left a political vacuum in the EC and as a result the limits of Economic and Monetary Union and its effects at a regional or local level have been left untouched.

Since the economic basis for the internal market has preceded the political and social basis, there are important questions about political accountability in the EC. This relates to the democracy deficit so frequently referred to in the political dimension of the EC. The main decision-making powers rest with the Council of Ministers. This is an unelected body, publicly unaccountable and secret, made up of representatives of member states' governments. To whom then is the Council of Ministers accountable? It is not accountable to national parliaments and the European Parliament and the Commission have too few powers to force any accountability. It has certainly not been accountable to women.

TOWARDS ECONOMIC AND MONETARY UNION AND POLITICAL UNION

In 1991 the Dutch Presidency of the European Council sought to take the EC forward in the most radical shake up of the EC since the signing of the Treaty in Rome. Two parallel Inter-Governmental Conferences on Economic and Monetary Union and European Political Union were held during 1991 with a view to discussing and signing the Luxembourg draft Treaty on Economic and Political Union. This culminated in the December 1991 Maastricht summit meeting. At the heart of the Inter-Governmental Conferences was the view that economic, social, environmental and political issues could no longer be left in the hands of national governments and that a single market would need a central European Bank and a single currency. Correspondingly it was also realised that EC decision-making should be shared more equitably between EC institutions and national, regional and local bodies.

Some of the poorer member states have argued forcefully for a large increase in resources for regional, economic and social policies if an agreement is to be reached on Economic and Political Union. Their demands are supported by the Commission but resisted by the UK government who consider social issues, in particular, to remain the realm of national governments.

The Luxembourg draft Treaty (Treaty of Union) proposed a complete overhaul of the Treaty of Rome. In the social policy chapter the draft Treaty updates the Treaty of Rome, consolidates many of the provisions found in the Social Charter and formalises them in EC law. On women's issues it amends Article 119 of the Treaty of Rome to include the provision that the equal pay principle 'shall not prevent any Member State from maintaining or adopting specific advantages in order to make it easier for women to pursue a vocational activity'. An amended Article 117 makes a specific reference to the need to introduce measures to fulfil the objective of promoting 'improved living and working conditions, proper social protection, the promotion of dialogue between management and labour, the development of human resources with a view to lasting high employment and the combatting of social exclusion'. This was couched in terms of measures that take account of diverse forms of national practices and the need to maintain competitiveness of the EC economy. The proposed amendment to Article 118 goes on to suggest the areas that the EC will support and complement member states' activities to include the working environment (particularly health and safety), working conditions, information and consultation of workers, equal opportunity in employment and equal treatment, as well as the vocational integration of people excluded from the labour market. To this end it was suggested that under certain conditions majority voting be used to introduce directives. For third country nationals provisions for social security and social protection of workers and access to employment could be introduced only by unanimous voting. It specifically excluded provisions relating to pay and the right of association or the right to strike. An important role was given to the dialogue between management and trade unions, both in the drawing up of new EC legislation and in its implementation. The draft Treaty also proposed EC action in education, training and youth through the development of greater cooperation between member states and the development of a vocational training policy.

While the draft Treaty gave an updated and wider-ranging profile to social policy, its progress was slowed down by lack of agreement over some key objectives by the UK. At the Maastricht summit in December 1991, the UK Government continued to voice its total opposition to the social chapter of the draft treaty on Political Union, in a similar vein to its opposition to the Social Charter in 1989. This led to the removal of the social chapter from the draft treaty, whose provisions formed a separate protocol that were agreed by the other eleven member states for implementation in 1993. The UK was once again isolated in its criticisms and left itself in a position of being able to opt out of decisions on key social issues if it so desired. This has left women in the UK in danger of falling further behind other member states, particularly since the protocol extended qualified majority voting to issues related to equality between men and women at work.

Here issues of national sovereignty have been used as a ploy to resist further social development taking place at the EC level, at a time when most member states are committed, at least in principle, to wider-ranging social objectives in the EC. This has particularly important implications for women and it is no surprise that the Inter-Governmental Conferences and the Maastricht summit have been, once again, dominated by male interests.

CONCLUSION

In developing policies for women in the context of the single market, the EC has moved on to a new stage of development. However, the policies developed have been fairly restrictive and have failed to give women the broad-based level of protection so urgently needed to ensure that women's unequal social and employment positions are not perpetuated. These policies, however, do little to address the specific forms of discrimination faced by disabled women, black, ethnic minority and migrant women and lesbians. They say nothing about women's unpaid work and women's roles as carers.

Moreover, channels of representation at the political level are in severe crisis, particularly in the regions of the EC where women are most disadvantaged. As a result of the growing calls to increase the powers of the European Parliament and to give greater political control to the regions there has erupted a new challenge to the democracy deficit that could also be engineered to give much better representation to women. The single market has prompted a heightened awareness amongst women that will not go away. The next chapter will look at the responses of women in trade unions and women's groups to the policies that have been developed and will show what their priorities are in the single market.

Notes

1. Under Articles 118a and 110a of the revised Treaty of Rome.
2. Under the new procedure the Council draws up a 'common position' on a proposal from the Commission, that takes account of amendments put forward by the Parliament in its first reading. Parliament can reject the 'common position' established by the Council by a majority of 260 (out of 518) votes or suggest new amendments through its new second reading powers. If it takes the second course of action the Commission can draw up a new proposal in the light of Parliament's amendments. The Council then has three months to vote on the new proposal, but this time with a qualified majority vote.

8 The Response of Trade Unions and Women's Groups: the Priorities for Women in the Single European Market?

WOMEN AND TRADE UNIONS IN EUROPE

Many of the priorities and actions facing trade unions in the single market are organised through the European Trades Union Confederation (ETUC), which provides a Europe-wide system of cooperation and a forum for the sharing of common problems. The run up to the completion of the internal market led to a much greater role for the ETUC in direct lobbying of the EC than had been evident in the past. Indeed, it has become an important forum for women in trade unions across Europe. Both through the Women's Committee and representation on the various Industry Committees in the ETUC, women have had a more visible and vocal presence in European trade union affairs.

Coordination of trade union activities throughout the EC is no easy task. This is hampered by different patterns of trade union organisation across Europe. Although coordinating bodies (union centres) exist in all EC countries, they are often organisationally different. National trade union centres only exist in the UK, Germany, Ireland and Greece. In other countries there is often more than one national or regional centre, or trade unions are organised along differing political lines.

However, developing closer ties with European unions is more problematic for women, not least because of their general under-representation in national unions. Table 8.1 shows the variations in women's union membership and their representation in top union positions in the 12 member states of the EC. In all countries women are under-represented in trade unions, especially in positions of leadership. It is only in Denmark that women's membership of trade unions matches their labour market participation. However, there has been a growth in women's union membership in most EC countries. This has increased the most in the unions representing workers in the public sector and retail trading. There has been a corresponding reduction in membership in unions covering women in the textile industry and declining industrial sectors.

Table 8.1   Women's involvement in European unions

Country	Union centre	Women union members (approx.) %*	Union general secretaries/ presidents %*
Belgium	CSC/FGTB	33	0
Denmark	LO/FTF	51	0
Spain	UGT/ELA-STV	16	11
France	CFDT/CGT-FO	32	9
UK	TUC	33	6
Greece	GSEE	25	4
Ireland	ITUC	32	0
Italy	CGIL/CISL/UIL	29	7
Luxembourg	CGT-LUX/LCGB	13	0
The Netherlands	FNV/CNV	18	13
Portugal	CGTP-IN/UGT	45	0
Germany	DGB	22	6
Total EC		29	5

* Figures do not include all union centres.

Source: Compiled from: ETUI, *Women and Trade Unions in Western Europe*, 1987, Labour Research Department, *Europe's Union Women*, March 1990.

In a survey carried out by Labour Research it was found that 'the trade union movement across the whole of the European Community is slowly moving to improve the position of women within its own structures and organisations' (LRD, 1990, p. 9). For instance, in 1989 the TUC created six extra seats on its general council. In Belgium a woman was appointed as general secretary of the FGTB union centre and the Italian CGIL introduced quotas for women. However, only in Germany and The Netherlands are women represented in union centres in similar proportions to their overall union membership.

Overall, only about five per cent of top positions in European unions are taken up by women.

The increase in union membership is a reflection of the greater participation of women in the labour market and corresponding attempts to recruit more women into unions, as overall union membership has declined. In Denmark over 50 per cent of working women are unionised, compared to between 30 and 33 per cent in the UK, Italy, Belgium and Ireland. In Germany the proportion of female membership is 22 per cent while in The Netherlands and Luxembourg this is 13 and 18 per cent respectively. These figures represent a significant increase in union membership, for instance, the proportion of women in UK unions rose from 28.5 per cent in 1978 to 32.4 per cent in 1988.

The growing representation of women in unions has brought with it an increase in the numbers of women's committees in trade union centres. Most union centres have national women's committees and/or departments with advisory functions and some have regional and local committees. Table 8.2 shows that women's committees are becoming more widespread within individual delegate unions at a national, regional and local level. They are slowly influencing union priorities

Table 8.2   Women's committees in national trade union centres

Belgium	CSC	Women's committees coordinated by two Trade Union Services for Women
	FGTB	Women's committees at national, regional and local levels
Denmark	LO	Standing Committee on Equality
	FTF	Equality Committee (Ligestillingsraadet)
Spain	UGT	Department for Women's Issues
	ELA/STV	No existing structure
France	CFDT	National Women's Committee
UK	TUC	Women's Committee
Greece	GSEE	No existing structure
Ireland	ICTU	Women's Committee
Italy	CGIL	Women's Advisory Committee
	CISL	Female Coordination Committee
Luxembourg	CGT-Lux	No existing structure
	LCGB	Separate women's organisation
The Netherlands	FNV	Women's Committee
	CNV	Women's Advisory Body
Portugal	UGT-P	Women's Committee
Germany	DGB	Women's Committee

and actions for equality programmes in, for instance, positive action for women, the greater representation of women in union hierarchies through quotas, and equality in collective bargaining. Despite attempting to introduce quotas in a number of unions, for instance in Belgium and Germany, these have been poorly implemented or unsuccessful. At the same time women are also often struggling to get women's issues onto national trade union agendas, whilst combining trade union work with full-time work and domestic responsibilities.

While some trade unions have national or union-based women's committees, others do not. All these factors place a strain on coordination at the European level and further problems for the institution of European wide collective bargaining in some industries that are likely to be particularly affected by the opening up of the internal market. In growing recognition of the need for European responses to bargaining the ETUC Women's Committee organised seminars on pay inequality between women and men in 1988 and 1989. It subsequently called for a European guide to job evaluation. It is evident that the interest shown amongst trade unions to women's issues in Europe has never been greater.

In many senses trade unions suffer from the lack of information relating to women and the single market, as do other groups. There is a general lack of information and understanding about what is feasible at the European level and to some extent European issues appear a long way from the reality of women's lives. However, women trade unionists are beginning to become much more informed about the single market, through national seminars and education programmes. For instance, the TUC held a seminar on 'Women and 1992' in May 1990, this provided an initial source of information that many women were able to take back to their own unions.

Other unions have begun to develop trade union education programmes around European issues. One problem facing many unions is that little time is available to discuss proposed EC legislation at a national, regional or local union level. The passage of many directives is too fast to enable intensive scrutiny by unions at the national level alone. This perpetuates the distance that many women feel exists between themselves and the policy-making environment in Brussels. At a European level there is a move towards developing Europe-wide seminars dealing with issues of common concern to trade unionists throughout Europe. The ETUC's European Trade Union College runs such seminars and is committed to developing a programme of seminars for women.

ETUC Women's Committee

The ETUC Women's Committee meets twice a year and is made up of representatives from all of the member union centres of the ETUC. Union centres with more than five million members can delegate three members and a representative from each of the ETUC's Industry Committees, but without voting rights. The president and vice-president of the Women's Committee are also members of the ETUC Executive Committee and have some voting rights. In 1990 there were only two women members of the Executive Committee from EC countries (a third woman member comes from Iceland). This is despite the passing of a resolution at the 1988 ETUC Congress calling on national union centres to increase the representation of women on ETUC bodies. The Women's Committee organises conferences and regularly sets up working parties to investigate particular problems or relevant issues. A Steering Committee also coordinates the work of the Women's Committee and meets regularly to implement decisions that are made. This is serviced by the secretariat of the Women's Committee and ensures its day-to-day running.

Of crucial concern to the Women's Committee has been the impact of the Single European Market on women workers. In particular it stresses the needs of the thousands of women throughout the EC who have little protection at work and who are often in the most vulnerable employment situations. It has been critical of EC policies that often stress the needs of middle-class skilled women, to the detriment of working-class women.

Slowly links are being developed between women in trade unions across Europe. In February 1991 the ETUC ran a women's seminar that brought women together from unions across Europe. Indeed it is apparent that women are increasingly seeking such contacts and are aware of the necessity for this to happen. This is facilitated at a formal level through the ETUC Women's Committee and at an informal level between women in different national unions. However, the ETUC Women's Committee secretariat spoke of the vital need for more links to be developed, but was hampered from doing this through lack of funding. Some interesting links have begun to develop with women working in border areas in the EC. For instance, women trade unions have established meetings and contacts in border areas in the north of Holland and the north of Germany as well as the borders in the south of Holland, the region of Aachen in Germany and the Belgian border with Germany. Likewise women trade unionists in various EC countries are planning European seminars.

It is apparent that some national trade union centres attach much greater importance to the role of the ETUC and its Women's Committee than others. The UK is seen to be one of the most active participants in the Committee and is also seen as the most aware of women's issues. The Dutch, the Danish and the Irish are also active but according to the secretariate: 'The British are the best and invest the most in the ETUC – thanks to Margaret Thatcher they became European' (interview, Beatrice Hertogs, 1990). However, there is a danger that trade unions are only using their links in Europe for specific gains and are avoiding taking a longer-term view of Europe; the UK, in this respect, has the most to gain from such an approach.

The priorities for women in the ETUC

In March 1990 the ETUC Women's Committee organised a meeting where a series of demands relating to the single market were made. These demands had some impact in the drawing up of the Commission's third action programme on equal opportunities. The demands were seen to be necessary in order that the single market should give women 'a new lease of life'.

One of the main priorities was action to prevent atypical work and on-call contracts leading to worsening employment conditions for women. As a result three directives were proposed relating to part-time work, temporary work, and homeworking and subcontracting. Although the EC Commission had proposed directives on part-time work and temporary working, it had not done so on homeworking. This had already been proposed by the Council of Europe and Dutch unions in 1989. It would involve giving homeworkers contracts of employment and the right to collective agreements, work inspection, social security and health and safety at work. Likewise no protection was given to the growing number of 'gangmasters' who recruit women for seasonal work, identified by the UK Transport and General Workers Union. The only Commission proposal that related to this was a Community policy on working conditions for those working in another member state, especially where they were subcontracted.

Strong priority was given to the demand for a directive on maternity rights. According to the Women's Committee: 'If there is an area, a matter of priority for the Women's Committee, which should be governed by the highest standards in the Community, then that area is maternity rights' (ETUC, 1990, p. 4). A directive on childcare was seen to be equally important and follows from the recommendation of the European Childcare Network. Likewise, the Committee also demanded that the European Regional Development Fund should take lack of childcare facilities into account in its decisions for co-funding, in the same way that it takes infrastructure, investment and local resources into account.

The reintroduction of the 1983 directive on parental and family leave was also demanded. This was on the basis that full-time or proportionally extended part-time parental leave provides a right to at least three months' leave (up to the child's second birthday or fifth birthday if the child is handicapped or adopted). Within this context it was argued that rights acquired should be retained, insurance benefits should be continued during the leave, the worker's job be guaranteed and that leave could be funded from public resources. Leave for family reasons was also seen as a right to a minimum number of paid days per year.

In the area of vocational training, it was recommended that half of the beneficiaries of the European Social Fund should be women, with childcare costs included in training costs. It was also suggested that national equal opportunities commissions and committees, in consultation with trade union women's bodies, should play a central role in determining the location and assessment of European Social Fund grants.

The Women's Committee also called for directives on individual rights to social security, the reversal of the burden of proof in equality cases, sexual harassment at work and positive action.

All of these recommendations went beyond the priorities set out in the Commission's Action Programme to implement the Social Charter and in the third action programme on equal opportunities. If implemented they would have a wider impact on women working in some of the most insecure and unprotected areas of work.

How far are women in trade unions ready for the Single European Market? A case study of trade unions in the UK

In 1990 a survey of trade unions in the UK was carried out by the author. It sought to assess how far trade unions were prepared for the single market and what policies they thought were important for women in the single market. The survey was based on questionnaires sent to national union women's officers and general secretaries who were represented on the TUC Women's Committee.

Many unions felt relatively unprepared for the single market and while there was some understanding of the issues at a national level, these were rarely understood or articulated at a local level. Moreover, it is apparent that women union members were largely ill-informed about the consequences that the single market could have on them. Some unions were actively seeking ways of rectifying this by developing more international union work on equality or by including the issue in union education programmes and issuing reports and information on women and Europe.

Some unions had developed their own checklists of questions for union negotiators in order to prepare them for negotiations with management on the issues relating to the single market. Many of the issues and questions covered were of direct relevance to women workers. A useful checklist had been developed by the TUC, and individual unions have developed their own. The Institute of Professionals, Managers and Specialists' checklist included issues relating to childcare, part-time work and racial discrimination, while the General Municipal, Boilermakers and Allied Union (GMB) checklist argued that:

> Each manager should welcome the opportunity to talk about their policy for 1992. Bad managers will try to avoid the issue. Many local managers may try to sidestep these questions and claim to be in the dark about top management's plans. So press very hard because unless we get the right answers GMB members may become sitting ducks in the 1992 shoot-out.

A number of unions felt hampered by a lack of information about the impact of the single market on women at a European level. Several unions have developed international departments with a special remit on Europe. For example, the Transport and General Workers Union has developed strategies for the internal market through its international department, including work on European equality issues. It was aware that the single market 'will be far ranging on our women's membership'. It organises large numbers of women in manufacturing and services, many of whom work in the industries that are sensitive to restructuring, including textiles, transport, chemicals, food, drink and tobacco, and public services.

Many unions felt that the EC had led to benefits for women since 1979, through the higher standards imposed on the UK from EC directives. However the Association of Cinematograph, Television and Allied Technicians saw that the Single European Act had led to 'retrogarde elements for some black women'. The Institute of Professionals, Managers and Specialists also argued that the 'problem of racial discrimination has been virtually ignored by the EC, while freedom of movement for non-EC nationals, including Commonwealth citizens in the UK, has been omitted from the Single European Act'.

Other unions had begun to develop strategies for dealing with the issues relating to the single market by developing publicity, reports and seminars to inform women. Some unions had held regular meetings on European strategy while others used their links with the ETUC to develop Europe-wide strategies. Several unions had not developed any specific strategies relating to the single market, and a larger number had done little or nothing specific to women. A few unions had developed national seminars for women members and some unions had developed policy statements.

Several unions had developed education packs and information for members. The Manufacturing, Science and Finance Union, for instance, had produced a pack entitled 'What about the workers? Europe 1992' and had run two schools on 'Women and 1992' with national and international speakers. The 1990 national women's conference of the Union of Shop, Distributive and Allied Workers was devoted to women and Europe. It argued that:

> Women in Britain probably have more to gain from 1992 than women in other countries in the Community. . . . Both the Social Charter and the standards set in the rest of Europe have given us something to aim at. From now on women in USDAW should be aiming to set European standards.

A report on women and Europe was also published for the conference. In addition the union produced an excellent workbook, *Europe 1992*, that included a section on women and 1992. The GMB had run a workshop on Europe at its 1989 Equal Rights Conference. Although it had produced an action guide on *Getting Ready for the European Social Charter*, it had not developed any specific documentation on women and the single market. The action guide recommended GMB representatives to use the Social Charter to press for rights for temporary and part-time workers; rights to information, consultation and participation in decisions about mergers, restructuring or new technology; improvements in training and education; improved child-care, parental leave and career breaks; and more union representation on workplace health and safety.

There was a general feeling expressed by all unions that women would face more disadvantages than advantages in the single market. The Manufacturing, Science and Finance Union saw that 'there could be problems if employers try to attract women in low-paid jobs, from one country to another. However, against this it should be possible to press for "best practice" in sex and equality cases'. Several unions identified particular problems for black women. However, it was anticipated that the EC would be of much greater importance to women in the UK if it continued to pass progressive legislation on women's equality. EC directives on equality issues were seen to be an important starting point for many unions. The National Union of Public Employees argued that the 'union will have increased bargaining power in negotiating to bring standards up to elsewhere in Europe'. Improved standards of health and safety and of maternity rights were viewed to be a positive effect by several unions.

Several unions felt that the single market would have a restricted impact on women but the UCATT argued that 'the arrival of increased numbers of better trained workers will push the chances of women receiving training even further back'.

All unions felt that further EC policies were necessary to ensure that women benefited from the internal market. The GMB saw that this was particularly important since 'we (in the UK) lag so far behind. Women don't share fully in prosperity even now, before 1992'. However, there was a general feeling that collective bargaining was the preferred course of action to improve women's rights. It was recognised that with such an anti-trade union government, the EC was the only hope for improvement for many women. The EC was also seen to be important for several unions since the UK fell behind higher standards in Europe. However, the Electrical Power Workers Association felt that the history of successive British governments did not offer 'much hope for equal opportunities in the 1990s'. The Manufacturing, Science and Finance Union was clear that 'if the Conservative Government remains in power, more policies are vital. In any case, European "best practice" is a target to aim for'. Several unions saw that it was essential to strengthen the Social Charter and to extend race discrimination laws to Europe as well as extending the law on disability to include anti-discriminatory law as exists in some US states. The National Union of Mineworkers saw this to be particularly important because of government opposition to a national minimum wage and equal rights for part-time workers and homeworkers.

All unions fully supported a Social Charter, but were critical of its lack of legal weight. Despite this there was a general feeling that the Charter could have some impact through the introduction of new directives, but that these would need to be strengthened and all of its provisions implemented. The UCATT argued that it would be 'a benefit to all workers and might improve the status of low-paid women's work'. NUCPS argued that 'given government policies on deregulation which could damage employment rights and maintain low pay, the social charter will be of benefit if it can introduce a degree of regulation'. Some unions were sceptical of the Government's Commitment to implement the charter fully. As a result the Fire Brigades Union stated that 'we need to maintain the momentum for change through trade unions'.

Unions were also asked to prioritise the most important issues facing women in the workplace in the 1990s. Many unions found that growing casualisation of work and the new forms of unprotected and atypical working patterns were important fronts for action. Childcare, parental leave, and maternity and paternity provisions were also high priorities. Other priorities included better trade union organisation and representation of women, pensions equality, training for women, action on low pay and changing social attitudes. All of these were seen to be increasingly important as priorities in the single market.

Many of the issues prioritised were considered to be equally important for EC action, particularly in setting minimum basic standards. In addition there was a concern that there was a need for EC action on race discrimination. While it was important for such action to take place at a local level as well, the EC was seen to be important in informing public opinion and changing attitudes.

Many unions were beginning to develop links with other unions and union organisations in Europe. For the most part these links were seen to rest with the ETUC and its relevant Industry Committees or the Women's Committee. Links with women working in the public sector had been made through the Public Services International, which organised a European Women's Seminar in Berlin in November 1990 where it anticipated that 'after 1992, especially during the

Transition Period, the Single Market could have an adverse impact on employment among women and increase the casualisation and marginalisation of women'. As a result it recommended that more protection should be given to women in collective bargaining for positive action, improved childcare, training and stronger EC legislation. Many unions were either planning or had developed links, information exchanges and visits with their counterpart unions in specific European countries. These contacts were seen as vital to develop understanding and cooperation that cut across national boundaries. Some unions had developed links between women in other European unions. For example, the Association of Cinematograph, Television and Allied Technicians had begun to develop contacts with women in film and television industries through a variety of bodies, as well as through the formal union channels.

Other unions had developed close links with Members of the European Parliament, for instance, in the coalfield communities. The Manufacturing, Science and Finance Union held regular meetings with women MEPs. Several unions had a direct link with the Women's Lobby and informal lobbying in Europe, while some unions had not established any links at all. It was recognised that there was a need for better representations and closer links in Europe, along with more lobbying through stronger links with the TUC and the ETUC.

Overall the survey found that unions were beginning to develop information, networking and lobbying strategies for women in the single market. It is evident that many unions saw the benefits of closer links in Europe due to the more positive policies emanating from the EC on women's rights. However, these policies were seen to be all the more necessary to protect women workers from competition in Europe.

PRIORITIES OF THE WOMEN'S COMMITTEE OF THE EUROPEAN PARLIAMENT

The Van Hemeldonck Report (committee on Women's Rights in the European Parliament, 1988) made a number of recommendations for women in the context of the internal market. One interesting recommendation was the setting up of a multidisciplinary unit in the Commission to monitor the impact of EC policies in employment, taxation, the social dimension, infrastructure and regional policy. This unit would make proposals for the reform of the structural funds to include special programmes for women living and working in the peripheral regions of the EC under the Regional Development Fund and with special priority for women's training under the European Social Fund.

The report also argued that the directives passed on equality were too weak to deal with the problems women face in the single market. As a result it was recognised that social and labour legislation needed to be extended to all women in the EC. It concluded that:

> All of these measures will prove only partially successful if the European Parliament, the Commission and the Council fail to make the women of Europe aware of the new dimension opening up fresh opportunities for them. European society and its institutions will undergo profound changes. This opportunity must be seized for providing a lasting and sound basis for women to play a full economic and political role in society. (European Parliament, 1988, p. 10)

PRIORITIES OF THE EUROPEAN WOMEN'S LOBBY: IS THERE SCOPE FOR MORE NETWORKING AMONGST WOMEN?

The European Women's Lobby

In July 1990 an initial work programme was discussed by the European Women's Lobby which included a number of agreed objectives. These were: monitoring the application of the equality directives in member states, pressurising the Commission and the Council of Ministers to adopt fully a comprehensive third equality action programme, and monitoring its implementation. It also argued that the introduction of the Social Charter should be monitored from the point of view of women and that directives that have been blocked in the Council of Ministers should be passed. Other lobbying initiatives included putting pressure on the Commission to encourage the sharing of work and family responsibilities, the protection of atypical jobs and the fight against poverty and social exclusion. It also recommended the setting up of a working group to look at the effects of the removal of border controls on migrant and ethnic minority women and an 'observatoire' to monitor women's representation in the media.

There is no doubt that the Women's Lobby is becoming an important vehicle for women's interests in the EC. Its work in representing women's interests in the single market is of crucial importance, although limited resources and uncertainty about priorities for action made it difficult to assess the importance of this influence in 1990. Nevertheless, it adds a new dimension of women's influence, so urgently needed to ensure that women are not marginalised or forgotten in the single market. It will certainly enhance the profile of women in the EC and will be a voice that cannot be ignored.

However, questions have been raised about the extent to which the Women's Lobby represents all women, especially at grass-roots level. The proposal for forming the Women's Lobby was initially opposed by the European Network of Women, which had developed a feminist network throughout Europe. It viewed that the initiative to set up a lobby from 'above' (the Commission), 'shows a serious deficit in democratic procedures which in turn, acts as a constant obstacle to the development of such lobby' (ENOW, 1989, p. 4). The Network was not consulted about the Lobby, despite its lobbying and networking activities at the European level since 1983. It has been critical of the Lobby's tight hierarchical structure and its failure to use the organisational principles of the women's movement across Europe.

As a result it recommended that three distinct groups should be represented, each keeping its own identity, priorities and structure. These would be first, feminist or grass-roots women's groups and organisations, second, traditional non-governmental women's organisations, and third, trade unions and women's committees of political organisations and groups. ENOW was clear that 'if the existing differences are not acknowledged, the lobby will run into the same difficulties that the Commission has been grappling with – when measures or laws proposed to improve the situation/position of women are opposed or vetoed by the Council of Ministers for political reasons' (ENOW, 1989, p. 4). Moreover, the organisation structure could lead to a top heavy structure that is undemocratic. There is a danger that the Lobby could become yet another EC institution, too distant from the women it is representing. According to ENOW, 'If the lobby pretends to be homogenous and assumes to represent the interests of all women, it will not be able to work effectively and will not be able to do the much needed political, innovative and pro-active work on behalf of women in the EEC' (ENOW, 1989, p. 5).

Other networks of women

Generally there is a feeling, especially at the national and regional level, that developments taking place in Europe are often too distant for women to influence. While the Women's Lobby may overcome some of these fears, it remains a tightly structured organisation that represents some of the more organised and established non-governmental women's bodies. Local authority women's committees, for instance, are not able to join the Lobby. In the UK women have been critical of the Lobby's under-representation of black women, lesbians and feminist groups.

As a result this is leading to the development of new networks of women across Europe, representing specific interests. Public and local authorities are increasingly having to integrate all aspects of EC policy into their own policy-making, and this includes women's policies. Women in local authorities are also keen to establish information networks of women across Europe to ensure that they too can have access to information to enable them to influence and lobby the EC around their specific interests. This has already begun with the National Association of Local Government Women's Committees in the UK, which is developing information and lobbying networks at a European, national and regional level. The plans for a Committee of the Regions, outlined in Chapter 6, could further strengthen this women's networking at a regional level.

Of equal importance is the need for local authorities to look at equal opportunities policies in the light of the impact of the internal market within their own region. Through the use of local and regional skills audits, it would be possible to identify women's training and childcare needs, and target resources appropriately. This can be tackled at the local or regional level and will be vitally important to enable women in the regions to lobby for the needs of their own regions, in a way that will be impossible for the European Women's Lobby to do.

It would be wrong to assume that one organisation could represent the interests of all women. The structure, organisation and limited resources of the Women's Lobby will mean that a European-wide system of lobbying will have objectives that will not be able to represent fully every region or every woman. However, it will be strategically placed to effect an important challenge to the EC policy-making system. Other networks will inevitably develop alongside the Lobby as specific demands and interests arise. One example of the development of a specific network has been the lauch of a women and poverty network through the European Network of Women. This has developed in response to the failure of the second and third EC poverty programmes to recognise women's poverty as an issue. It follows the successful tribunal on women and poverty held in Brussels in 1989, where women living in poverty spoke of their own experiences. It involved women at a grass-roots level, something that has remained a long-standing objective of the Network. During 1990–1 a series of transnational meetings was organised in various European cities and a programme of research is under way to target key areas of action and information on women's poverty.

Black and ethnic minority women

At another level black and ethnic minority women are forming their own networks and are beginning to lobby the EC institutions. In Jane Goldsmith's report (1990) on the effects of the internal market on black and ethnic minority women in the UK, a number of recommendations are made for the representation of black and ethnic minority women in the policy-making process. These include the coordination of research on black and ethnic minority women in the EC and the representation of the multicultural nature of European society in all EC publications and reports. It was also recommended that policies to protect black workers be drawn up, for instance in protecting homeworkers. Likewise it was seen to be important to monitor the EC's activities by race and gender, with priority for ethnic minority women in the European Social Fund and other funding programmes. The report also called for more representation of black women in EC decision making and more consultation of black and ethnic minority groups at the grass-roots level. Finally, it recommended that non-EC nationals should be allowed free movement in the EC and the need for an 'open, democratic debate about immigration policy issues within the EC for Third Country Nationals'.

Other types of networking are developing both formally and informally at other levels. The discussion above about women and trade unions shows that attempts at networking across Europe have begun. Formal equal opportunities commissions and committees across Europe, who meet through the Commission's Advisory Group, are also looking at ways in which they can network outside the formal EC institutional structure.

CONCLUSION

This chapter has outlined some of the main priorities for women in the single market. It has also shown how far unions in the UK are preparing for the impact of the single market on women members.

The information and lobbying networks developing amongst women in Europe now work on a scale that has never been witnessed before. They are setting up new priorities for women in the Single European Market that demonstrate that women do not want to be left on the sidelines of European integration. They are establishing their own priorities for action that are based on women's real needs and experiences and are increasingly at the forefront of change in the EC.

9 Conclusion: Towards a Feminist Analysis of the European Community

Women in the EC face both different and similar problems in their access to the Single European Market. It is clear that in all EC countries women share experiences of exploitation and marginalisation at work. Their lives are constrained by national social policies that continue to reflect their dependence on men and their subordinate positions in all aspects of European society. Women's weaker position in the labour market was discussed in Chapter 2, where it was shown that women's strengths and contributions to work and the family are undervalued. Large numbers of women work in poorly paid and atypical forms of employment. Their access to childcare, training and skilled jobs is similarly constrained by policies that assume their dependence in the family, in contradiction to economic demands for their greater integration into work.

What is evident is that women start from a weaker position to compete for the better-paid and skilled jobs promised in the single market. These issues were discussed in Chapter 3 where it was suggested that without adequate compensatory measures, women will be the losers rather than the winners in the single market. This is particularly the case for women working in jobs that are sensitive to restructuring, women living in the peripheral regions of the Community, women with poor access to training and skilled work, and for black and ethnic minority women.

A number of important policy developments have taken place for women at the EC level. This book has assessed how the development of policy has led to improvements for women in the EC, particularly in relation to the Single European Market. It has discussed who has been influential in determining policy, the perspectives brought to the policy-making table and the social, economic and political environment in which policy making takes place. It has also focused on the role of interest groups and the representation and promotion of women's interests in this process. These have been constrained both by the institution of patriarchy and by the resulting actions of male-dominated policy-making which have influenced and determined the development and scope of policy.

An assessment of the nature of both EC and national policy-making has demonstrated an important relationship between the two. This takes place at several levels, with the EC affecting policy at the national level in two ways and the member states affecting the EC process in a further two ways. Each of these factors affects the final outcome of policy and the way in which it is implemented. They are as follows:

1. EC law has overridden national law and this has resulted in the member states being required to respect both Article 119 and the subsequent directives on equality.
2. EC policy has been imaginative in persuading employers and national governments of the necessity to develop wider legal provisions, not least in the way in which women have been seen as an untapped resource for change. Its educative role has been important in this context.
3. Member states have been involved in the negotiation and determination of the final outcome of EC policy in Brussels. For instance, UK resistance to extend women's rights beyond the existing legislative framework has been carried over into the EC policy-making process.
4. Member states have been able, to an extent, to determine the implementation of EC policy at the national level.

At all levels it is evident that patriarchy plays a key role in determining the outcome and subsequent implementation of policy.

EC policy in favour of women has developed in four stages. Chapters 5 and 7 discussed the factors that led to a widening of the scope of the EC's policy on women. The different institutions of the EC and the EC policy-making structure were also looked at in Chapter 4 in order to demonstrate the various ways in which women's interests have been mobilised and articulated. From this it became apparent that EC policy has developed out of a complex political process involving the EC institutions, national governments and a whole variety of different groups who have, to a greater or lesser degree, influenced the process.

EC policy has shifted in focus over the four stages of development. The first stage (1957–69) was primarily economic and equal pay was included to prevent a competitive disadvantage for one member state. Little progress was made in implementing equal pay since it was found not to lead to higher social costs. Article 119 provided an important principle that overrides national law and while strict in focus has been used as a catalyst for more far-reaching measures.

The second stage of development (1970–9) saw the EC responding to a need to move away from its exclusively economic focus towards one that prioritised social policy, in particular action for women. This stage ended with the Commission taking a more direct role in securing implementation through the issuing of infringement proceedings against member states who had failed to implement the equal pay directive.

By the time the EC reached the third stage (1980–6), economic crisis halted the progressive development of policy in the Council of Ministers. Nevertheless, the third stage saw an imaginative and wide-ranging set of measures being discussed by the European Parliament and the Commission, who responded to the need to incorporate women's interests into the development of EC policy. These measures, including the rights of part-time workers, positive action and parental leave, looked more closely at the structural limitations to equal pay. The UK, in particular, was opposed to any extension of policy that would improve the situation of women and displayed hostility to such proposals in the Council of Ministers.

The fourth stage of development (1986–92) took the Community into a new era of change. The passing of the Single European Act and the development of policy after 1986 were geared to ensuring that a 'social dimension' became an integral part of the internal market. Here women became more vocal in their demands for more far-reaching policies.

It is clear that as the EC moved through the different stages of development, political changes altered the nature of European integration. Once committed to equal pay the member states were forced to abide by the EC's policies and to agree to further directives to counter the disadvantages women faced in the labour market. By the third stage this, however, had taught the reluctant Council of Ministers, concerned about EC and national budgets, to restrict the extent of legislation, whilst maintaining a minimal degree of support for women's employment, by passing non-binding resolutions (most notably in the setting up of the two Action Programmes in the 1980s). Thus, the development of the EC's women's policy has been closely related to the economic and social priorities of member states.

At some levels, a broader set of policies has developed in the EC, most notably within the Commission and the Parliament, in response to wider feminist demands and the growing use of feminist research to inform policy development. The scope of the debate about the position of women and sexual divisions within the labour market and the home has significantly widened. Women's interests gained a much wider hearing at the EC level after the first stage. The Commission and the Parliament welcomed this support for their policies and women's groups have been useful allies in pushing for further developments. In this respect, they have encouraged an open framework in their policy-making activities and their role in agenda setting. They have attempted to create 'issue communities' of support for their policy proposals, through the organisation of seminars, conferences and lobbying. Moreover, the responsiveness of both the Commission and the Parliament to 'intellectual innovation', particularly in the use of research, has led to the initiation of new policy proposals. Many of these have been informed by feminist theory, and have begun to recognise the deep-seated and structural nature of the inequalities that women face in the labour market.

However, Commission- and Parliament-initiated policy proposals have received little positive reaction within the Council of Ministers, which has stuck fast to unchanging patriarchal relations. National states, employers and other powerful groups have maintained a sufficient degree of control to limit the potentially progressive aspects of EC policy in this area. In this sense the make-up of national policy-making and of political ideologies remains of crucial importance to this process. As a result a number of problems have presented themselves as policy has developed incrementally. First, the EC policy-making structure has been affected by changing economic, political and social priorities. This has led to piecemeal developments that have at times been lacking in continuity. This has thwarted the merits of incrementalism, made possible by the exhorting and catalytic nature of many of the Treaty provisions.

Second, the EC has become increasingly diversified, representing a large block of countries with very different socioeconomic, political and cultural traditions. EC policy has been seen to have the effect of bringing countries with poorer legal standards for women up to the EC standard, rather than developing still wider policy provisions for women in the more advanced member states. The potential for an even wider group of countries to include some of the European Free Trade Association members and those of Eastern European countries will further enhance these differences. As a result it has become increasingly important to find balance and agreement between the more advanced and the less advanced member states. Equally important are the different traditions and approaches to women's rights in member states. While this had led to differences in approach at the national level, it is evident that women in all EC countries share common problems and experiences. Nevertheless, the differences in government approaches does mean that it is unlikely that there will be a uniform pattern of women's policies in all member states.

This is a particularly important issue for women in the single market since policies to facilitate the free movement of labour, the harmonisation of policies and measures to prevent social dumping are necessary if women are not to be further disadvantaged from competition, rationalisation and new forms of trade in Europe. These necessitate the development of uniform minimum rights, designed to protect women and ensure their integration and reintegration into work. Attempts to harmonise and standardise EC provisions have led to difficulties for the Commission. Likewise, the differing political ideologies of member states have led to difficulties in reaching agreement and compromise in the Council of Ministers, crucial for extending the EC's women's policy.

Third, there are problems relating to the areas of EC competence and the question of subsidiarity. Although most of the measures passed have no direct legal reference in the Treaty of Rome, EC policy has been imaginative in its use of Article 119 of the Treaty. However, it has become increasingly difficult to draw the line at which responsibilities lie with member states and which with the EC. As a result this question of subsidiarity continues to raise problems in the determination of new policy areas. It is equally used as an excuse for not embarking on some of the more controversial aspects of policy that women have demanded, for example, binding measures on childcare, parental leave, positive action and maternity rights.

Fourth, the policy-making system in the EC has been faced with a 'democracy deficit' and this has been restricted by the limited powers given to both the Parliament and the Commission in determining final outcomes to policy. This became more evident in the run-up to the single market, where questions of political accountability have been raised at the regional and national levels.

Finally, it is clear that the EC has a limited role in ensuring that member states fulfil their obligations under EC law, particularly in the implementation of the directives. There are no sanctions available to the Commission, other than the lengthy procedure involved in taking a member state to the European Court of Justice. This lack of sanction over implementation has led to significant problems for the Commission.

In this light Chapter 6 assessed the impact of the EC's policy in the UK. This gave some insight into the problems of implementation at the national level, which provides some important lessons for the implementation of policies in the single market. Time lags mean that policy is very slow to reach implementation into national legislation, often cumbersome and fraught with difficulties. Moreover, the practical application of EC policy on equal pay in the UK, while widening the scope of the law, had a number of structural limitations. This was shown in the role of the Government in minimising the potentially broad effects of the introduction of equal value and the rejection of wider policy proposals. Despite the negative attitude of the UK Government to widening the scope of equal pay, it was shown that the EC's policy has led to important legislative gains for women in the UK.

The amendment to the Equal Pay Act in 1984, however, was carried out in a way that minimised the full impact of equal value. Consultations with various interest groups resulted in the Government being pressurised into removing some of the more negative aspects of its proposals. This was particularly important since the methods for introducing an amendment failed to provide for democratic debate and parliamentary scrutiny. The UK Government's role in implementing the wider provisions of EC law has been characterised by reluctance and hostility. In EC policy-making the Government has been primarily concerned with narrow nationalistic issues and the protection of producer interests.

Thus, the introduction of equal pay for work of equal value, while a breakthrough for women, remains problematic. This is because it has been up to employers and unions to facilitate the application of equal value. While the policy developed by the EC may have been progressive, its implementation in the UK has been characterised by patriarchal relations. Nevertheless, the evidence from the two surveys carried out for this study suggests that trade unions have utilised the equal value provisions imaginatively. In those trade unions where women's interests are increasingly being felt, equal value has been implemented in a more positive way than was initially expected.

The role of trade unions in developing policies and preparing themselves for the single market was discussed in Chapter 8. Here it was found that trade unions at a European and national level are gradually developing their own strategies, priorities and actions for women in the single market. This is an important development in the light of the greater emphasis placed on the role of the 'social partners', in the creation of a corporatist structure to policy making in the EC. Social developments in the EC are often only seen in the context of competing producer interests. Accordingly, policies have been closely related to the supply and cost of labour. Such a framework has implications for the scope of policy developments. It has been clear that growing pressure from women has ensured a greater focus of women's interests in policy-making. Nevertheless, the powerful producer interests have thwarted these less powerful influences.

EC legislation and its implementation in member states has had the effect of making illegal some of the more overt and direct forms of discrimination that make women's access to jobs and pay unequal. Whilst such an approach has led to some improvements, it is clear that unless legislation is backed up with strong implementation measures, a legislative framework will essentially be limited. For instance, there has been a failure to challenge fully the effects of family ideology, sexual divisions in the labour market, the organisation of work and of trade unions, and the exploitation of women who will continue to service the population and make it ready and fit for work and to care for those who can no longer work. Policies have also been based on the need for larger numbers of women to work, though not always in skilled work. These take for granted women's unpaid work in the home or in the family enterprise, as well as women's domestic and caring roles.

Increasingly black feminists are also showing the ways in which social policies are also structured by 'race' as well as gender. An understanding of racial and sexual divisions shows how the exploitation of black people and women is tied up with racial domination and female subordination.

In many senses the EC's policies provide little more than a framework for equal opportunities. This development of policy has largely failed to tackle either the material or the structural roots of women's oppression and inequality. The marginalisation of women's interests in policy-making has been evident precisely because both capitalism and patriarchy derive material benefit from the disadvantaged position of women in society.

Despite this, women have been influential in organising their interests and pressurising for change, in response to EC policy at both the national and EC level. This was discussed in Chapters 4 and 8. Indeed, it has been in response to women's pressure that policy has been developed at both the national and the EC level in the first place, although it is clear that this has faced limitations.

It has been shown that women have been more conscious of the gains that can be made from EC membership than was evident in the early days of the EC. Women's expectations of the EC have been raised and women's interests have a voice in both the policy-making and implementation processes.

An enormous body of law, information and networking has resulted from the development of EC policies. Women's groups, pressure groups and trade unions have increasingly focused on the EC for the change that would not have been possible at the national level. They have sought reforms and wider-ranging policies from the EC, rather than from national governments. They have injected a new set of demands to ensure that women are not marginalised in the single market, and that their experiences of racism and sexism are taken seriously.

This is no easy task since the world of international and European politics has long been the territory of men:

> So far feminist analysis has had little impact on international politics. Foreign-policy commentators and decision makers seem particularly confident in dismissing feminist ideas, Rare is the professional commentator on international politics who takes women's experiences seriously. (Enloe, 1989, p. 3)

As women have developed cross-national links by meeting at the European level to make demands on the EC they have at some levels begun to articulate a feminist critique of the male club of European decision-making. Without a feminist analysis it is impossible to show how patriarchy shapes the very make-up of the EC and its subordination of women. Campaigns need to be directly related to women's real experiences at work, in the home and in their local communities. Without a feminist analysis, women will be left wondering what the EC is all about and how it will affect them, rather than being drawn into the centre of an analysis of why Europe is structured in the way that it is and how change can realistically be to their benefit.

The Single European Market is based on the transformation of capitalist economics onto a wider European scale. At its core is the exploitation of women. It is also based on the need for larger numbers of women to work, though not always in skilled work. It takes for granted women's unpaid work in the home or in the family enterprise, as well as women's domestic and caring roles.

One issue facing women in the development of policies in the single market is that rights derived at a time of labour shortages could be short-lived. Because women's employment has coincided with the introduction of the single European market there is a danger that rights will only be developed to facilitate the entry of larger numbers of women into the labour market. During times of labour shortage or national emergency or war women have been brought into the labour market. Social policies, like the provision of childcare, have helped to encourage the greater participation of women into paid work. But rights to childcare have often been removed when women are no longer needed in the labour market. Unless these rights become established as permanent, undisputed and free-standing, they too could be at risk. For this reason there is a need for strong legal measures that will establish rights which cannot easily be taken away at the whim of economic change. There is also a need for women's interests to be represented amongst political elites in Europe. Christine Crawley (MEP) has called for a Commissioner for Women for this very reason.

The scope and concept of discrimination also needs clarifying at the EC level. The European Parliament has called for a Community definition of equality of opportunity and discrimination: 'past and present Commission approaches have not been consistent . . . with some groups being excluded from access to programmes or excluded from statements of values without due explanation or reason' (European Parliament, 1990c). It has recommended that the Commission's anti-discrimination work should automatically include women, black and ethnic minority people, people with disabilities, including learning disabilities, lesbians and gay men, and older and younger people. Also needed is a recognition of discrimination on the grounds of religion and political belief, and of responsibilities for caring for others, all of which must be integrated into the development and monitoring of all Community policies, so that women are not, once again, left on the sidelines of change and progress.

Europe with a single market has the potential to address more wide-ranging policies for women, that have hitherto remained untouched. Although the Treaty established constitutional guidelines on what can be achieved in EC policy, there is nothing preventing its further amendment if all member states agree to it. Thus issues which have not been of concern to a common market could have increasing importance in the single market. These will include further pressure for the harmonisation of social benefits and social protection and policies relating to the trafficking of pornography. There is a much greater potential for policies relating to violence against women and sexual abuse in the context of free movement of labour.

The single market cannot rely on economic policy for the future development of Europe. Social policies will be vital to ensure that competition does not leave one region or one group of people in a disadvantaged position. There will be a much greater need to take account of the proposals from the networks of women that are developing at a regional and European level and of the proposals of the women's committees of the European Parliament and the ETUC. These are not glib demands, they are real demands for the integration of a Europe that recognises difference and inequality, and the rights of all women to benefit from the single market.

Rather than just responding to the EC's policies, women need to be at the centre of the debate about the single market and its effect on women. The women's movement will increasingly have to look at campaigns to extend women's rights with a European and international focus, rather than a national focus, as more policies are deliberated at the European level. They need to be able to assert their own particular needs in a political environment that understands and recognises their demands. Lobbying from the outside will be insufficient to change the make-up of political elites in the short term, but may influence the debate and representation of women in these elites in the long term. A feminist analysis of the EC needs to take these issues on board. It requires an understanding of the nature and role of patriarchy and of women's paid and unpaid roles in work in the development of the EC. Economic policies need to be closely integrated with social policies that represent all women, including single parents, lesbians, single women, black and ethnic minority women, old women, young women and disabled women. It is only with an understanding of sexual and racial divisions in European society that women can be brought to the centre of the debates about the single market. Only then can women's interests be taken seriously.

Appendix 1: Institutions of the European Community

European Community policy-making takes place in a variety of institutional settings. Each institution has its own powers and responsibilities laid down in the Treaty of Rome. Figure A.1 shows the relationship of the institutions of the EC to each other and to the national policy making process, and the roles that each institution has in the development of legislation.

THE COMMISSION

The Commission, based in Brussels, exists to 'ensure the proper functioning and development of the common market' (Article 155). It is headed by 17 Commissioners, nominated by national governments. Each Commissioner is responsible for one area of EC policy. The Commissioner for Employment and Social Affairs has overall responsibility for policies affecting women at work. The Commission is also expected to promote and develop new policies, under Article 100 of the Treaty of Rome. This enables the Commission to propose to the Council of Ministers new legal instruments for harmonising the laws of member states. It also acts to ensure that member states implement EC law. As a result the Commission is empowered to initiate proceedings before the Court of Justice if member states fail to implement the measures necessary to bring national law in line with Community law (Articles 169 and 171).

THE COUNCIL OF MINISTERS

This is the power base of the Community, where all major decisions are made and where policies affecting women are either rejected or accepted. It is here that the EC's most powerful actors, notably national governments, are represented. It has reproduced and reinforced male interests, and is the most patriarchal of all the institutions. It is only occasionally that women's interests are directly represented. Yvette Roudy from the French Ministry of Women's Rights was an avid proponent of women's interests during the 1980s in a reluctant and male-dominated Council of Ministers.

The presidency of the Council of Ministers is rotated between the different member states every six months. As a result the attitude of the presidency in office towards women's rights directly affects the setting of the agenda in the Council of Ministers' meetings. Member states, reluctant to extend women's

Figure A.1   The institutions of the EC, their relationships to each other and to the national policy-making process

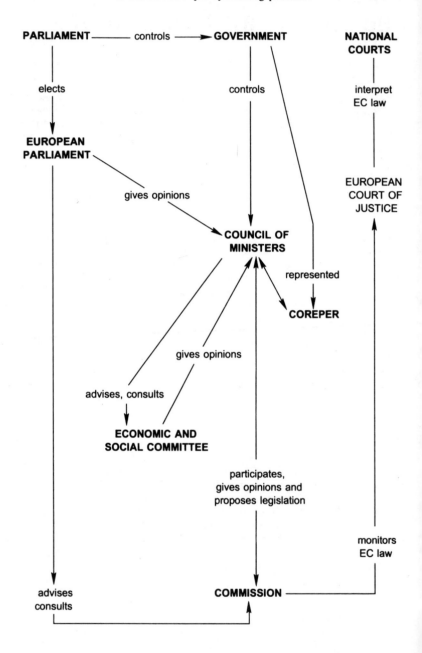

rights, have used their presidencies to block the discussion of proposals, while member states keen to see the swift advancement of policy have given women's issues a higher priority on the agenda. This was evident both with the Irish and Italian presidencies during 1990.

The Council of Ministers exists to ensure that the objectives set out in the Treaty of Rome are attained (Article 145). It makes decisions on legislation that is proposed by the Commission and seeks the opinions of the European Parliament and the Economic and Social Committee on draft legislation. It consists of representatives of national governments, who vary according to the subject discussed. The Employment Minister, for example, will represent the government in the Council of Ministers if some aspects of women's employment are being discussed. Meetings in the Council of Ministers are typified by long, heated discussions where bargaining and package deals are often the only way in which a decision is made.

Of particular importance was the introduction, in 1987, of a system of decision making to facilitate the speedy passage of internal market legislation through the Council of Ministers. This shifted the bulk of the work on the completion of the internal market over to majority voting, although key areas of social policy remained subject to unanimity.

A great deal of bargaining, compromise and cooperation between member governments takes place within COREPER, the Committee of Permanent Representatives. It is made up of representatives of national governments and assists the Council of Ministers and the vast array of working groups that now exist in policy formulation. While the greater role now given to COREPER enables consensus to be achieved in a more efficient way, public accountability is limited to that exercised through national government representations.

Finally, as the Community has progressed, and, as the determination of policy has become more complex, more functions regarding the overall direction of the EC are deliberated in the now permanently established European Council. This is carried out through regular summits attended by the heads of governments of all member states. The role of the Council of Ministers, COREPER and the European Council ensures that important and sensitive national political questions are raised in the determination of broad policy goals. Indeed these may not always have a European focus to them. The powerful expression of national interests is, however, contained at times in attempts to hold the Community together.

THE EUROPEAN PARLIAMENT

The European Parliament is the parliamentary body of the EC and by its nature is political and democratic. It was developed as a body to legitimise Community activities and is described in the Treaty of Rome as 'representing the peoples of the states' in addition to acting 'to exercise the advisory and supervisory powers' (Article 137).

Although directly elected, the European Parliament has remained a consultative rather than a legislative body, despite being given more powers in 1987. It does not hold the same constitutional basis, power and authority that national parliaments hold. Its formal legislative role is limited to placing political pressure on the Commission to implement policies it considers to be important, and suggesting amendments and giving opinions to the Council of Ministers. In addition, it has a number of budgetary powers and works with the Council of Ministers to determine the annual budget. It also exerts a degree of political, democratic and executive control over the Commission and the Council. The function of political control is enshrined in the ultimate power to sack the Commission. This ensures political accountability along with the requirement that the Commission addresses oral and written questions, submits reports (including its annual report) and takes part in parliamentary debates and committee meetings.

While the European Parliament has limited legislative authority, its influence has been most evident in getting the Commission to adopt new proposals. It can also be influential in pressurising the Commission to amend its proposals in the light of amendments and opinions suggested by the Parliament. These can then only be rejected by a qualified majority in the Council of Ministers.

The first direct elections to the European Parliament, in 1979, brought with them increasing pressure from within the Parliament and from the electorate, to increase its legislative powers. Ultimately the powers of the Parliament depend on the actions of member governments. From the start some member states have seen the Parliament as having only a consultative role (the UK and Denmark). Others (the Dutch, Germans and Italians) have sought to strengthen Parliament's participation in legislation in order to compensate for the loss of power of their own national parliaments.

THE ECONOMIC AND SOCIAL COMMITTEE

This is an advisory body and a part of the EC institutional structure. It is consulted on a designated range of issues, including those concerning women's employment and pay. It is made up of representatives of national interest groups, known as the social partners. In practice these have tended to be workers' and employers' organisations, who have been incorporated into the policy making structure. Its powers are limited to giving advice and opinions to the Council of Ministers. The 1972 Paris Summit sought to improve relations with the Council, granting the Committee the right to issue opinions on its own initative. The setting up of the Standing Committee on Employment in 1974, however, did focus much attention away from the Economic and Social Committee on employment-related issues.

In its proposals on European union, the Economic and Social Committee called for a European Economic and Social Council that was not just a consultative body, but rather an assembly representing organised economic and social interests at the European level. While attempting to strengthen the role of the Economic and Social Committee this would have resulted in the relationship between the Council and Commission with the European Parliament being substantially weakened.

THE EUROPEAN COURT OF JUSTICE (ECJ)

The ECJ exists to clarify and interpret EC law and to ensure that member states apply the requirements of the Treaty (Article 164). As a court it makes decisions based on cases brought either by national governments, individuals or the EC Commission under Articles 169 and 171 of the Treaty of Rome. EC law is made up of primary legislation, found in the Treaty, and secondary legislation which is based on and develops out of the Treaty provisions. The ECJ is made up of 13 judges who are appointed by national governments, and six Advocates-General who give impartial advice on cases brought before the ECJ.

National courts are able to ask the ECJ for a preliminary ruling on the interpretation of Community law. Rulings by the Court have led to several important extensions to women's rights in the member states in equal pay, sex discrimination and social security. National courts are also bound by EC law to follow judgments and rulings that are made by the Court and this has the effect of ensuring that the law is applied in a uniform way. For example, the Commission initiated a number of infringement proceedings against member states who failed to implement the 1975 Directive on Equal Pay. In the case of the UK the Court upheld the Commission's complaint and this led to an amendment to the 1970 Equal Pay Act, in 1984, to bring it in line with the directive.

Appendix 2: How Can Women Influence the EC Process?

There are a number of ways in which women can influence the decision-making process both within the institutions of the EC and also through networks that have developed outside them.

COMMISSION OF THE EUROPEAN COMMUNITIES

200 rue de la Loi, 1049 Brussels.

● Equal Opportunities Unit, in DG V, (Directorate General for Employment, Industrial Relations and Social Affairs). Draws up new proposals and monitors EC legislation on women. Coordinates the Advisory Group on Equal Opportunities and the networks of experts (below).

● Advisory Group on Equal Opportunities for women (made up of representatives of equal opportunities commissions and committees, represented in the UK by the Equal Opportunities Commission. The Group advises the Commission's Equal Opportunities Unit on new legislation.

● Networks of experts are attached to DG V and offer advice for new policies as well as monitoring the implementation of EC policies in member states. The networks cover the following areas: childcare, the diversification of occupational choices, women in the labour market, the implementation of equality directives, equal opportunities in education, women in local employment initiatives, women in higher and public service, women in industry, IRIS network on vocational training and equal opportunities in broadcasting. Each network has at least one national representative.

● Women's Information Unit, DG X (Directorate General for Information, Communication and Culture). Publishes the free bimonthly *Women of Europe*, coordinates the role of women's groups throughout Europe and provides information to women on policy developments.

Information can also be gained through the London Office of the Commission, 8 Storey's Gate, London SW1P 3AT.

EUROPEAN PARLIAMENT

Women's Committee Secretariat, Plateau de Kirchberg, Luxembourg.

● Women's Committee – made up of representatives of all political groups in the Parliament. Carries out own initiative reports on a wide range of topics and places considerable pressure on the Commission to draw up new policies for women. The Committee is chaired by Christine Crawley, MEP.

EUROPEAN TRADE UNION CONFEDERATION

37 rue Montagne aux Herbes Potagères, 1000 Brussels.

● Women's Committee – representatives from trade union centres throughout Europe. Lobbies the Commission and runs seminars. It produced a list of demands for women in the Single European Market in May 1990.

CENTRE FOR RESEARCH ON EUROPEAN WOMEN

38 rue Stevin, 1040 Brussels.

● CREW provides women throughout Europe with regular information through CREW reports and carries out research for both the Commission and women's organisations in Europe. It coordinates the highly successful IRIS network on women's training programmes.

EUROPEAN NETWORK ON WOMEN

c/o Castleford Women's Centre, 2 Wesley Street, Castleford, West Yorkshire WF10 1AE

● A feminist-based organisation that has developed links with women throughout all EC countries. It lobbies the EC institutions and runs conferences and seminars. For instance in 1988 it ran a tribunal on women and poverty in Brussels.

EUROPEAN WOMEN'S LOBBY

Jacqueline de Groote, 11 avenue de Mercure, Bte 4, 1180 Brussels.

● The European Women's Lobby was set up to represent women's interests throughout the EC. It is made up of representatives of European and national women's organisations (individuals cannot be members) and it held its first general assembly in Brussels in September 1990. It is setting up an office and secretariat in Brussels and will lobby the EC to develop more legally binding measures for women as well as to monitor progress in individual member states.

EUROPEAN FORUM OF SOCIALIST FEMINISTS

● An organisation of socialist feminists across Europe. Holds an annual conference.

STANDING CONFERENCE ON RACIAL EQUALITY IN EUROPE

c/o House of Commons, London SW1.

● Pressure group set up by Berni Grant, MP, to raise the issue of racial discrimination in the EC and to press the EC to adopt anti-discrimination legislation.

Appendix 3: European Community Legislation in Favour of Women

The Treaty of Rome makes it possible for new legislative provisions to be made under Article 100 and Article 235 of the Treaty. These include regulations, directives, decisions, opinions and recommendations, and resolutions. They vary in their enforcement and legal weight and the extent to which national implementing measures need to be introduced. EC legislation relating to women is listed below.

REGULATIONS

These introduce new law that overrides national law. There have been no proposals for legislative action in this area.

DIRECTIVES

These are binding, but require member states to implement national provisions to achieve the objectives of the directive. Directives that have been passed or proposed include:

● Council Directive 75/117/EEC of 10 February 1975 on the approximation of the laws of member states on the application of the principle of equal pay for men and women. *Offical Journal* L 45, 19.2.75, p. 19.
● Council Directive 76/207/EEC on the implementation of the principle of equal treatment for men and women as regards access to vocational training and promotion, and working conditions. *Official Journal* L 39, of 14.1.76, p. 40.
● Council Directive 77/804/EEC on action by the European Social Fund for women. *Official Journal* L 337, 27.12.77.
● Council Directive 79/7/EEC on the progressive implementation of the principle of equal treatment for men and women in matters of social security of 19 December 1978. *Official Journal* L 6, 10.1.79, p. 24.
● Council Directive 86/378/EEC on the implementation of the principle of equal treatment for men and women in occupational social security schemes. *Official Journal* L 225, 12.8.86.

● Council Directive 86/613/EEC on the application of the principle of equal treatment between men and women engaged in an activity, including agriculture, in a self-employed capacity, and on the protection of self-employed women during pregnancy and motherhood. *Official Journal* L 359, 19.12.86.

● Proposed Council Directive on parental leave and leave for family reasons. Commission of the European Communities (1984) *Proposal for a Directive on Parental Leave* COM (83) 686 final, *Official Journal* C333, 9.12.83, pp. 6–8. Submitted to Council of Ministers on 24 November 1983. Amended proposals on 15 November 1984, COM (84) 631 final, *Official Journal* C316, 27.11.84, pp. 7–9. Stalemate since then.

● Proposed Council Directive on completion of equal treatment in social security, covering pension age, survivor's benefits and family allowances, submitted by the Commission to Council on 27 October 1987, blocked since then. COM (87) 494 final, *Offical Journal* C309, 19.11.87, pp. 10–13.

● Proposed Council Directive on the burden of proof in discrimination cases, submitted by the Commission to the Council on 27 May 1988, vetoed by UK in 1989. *Official Journal* C176, 5.7.86, p. 5.

● Proposed Council directive on the approximation of laws relating to working conditions, regarding the rights of workers with atypical work contracts (e.g., part-time work, temporary work etc). Based on Commission proposal of 13 June 1990, COM (90) 228.

● Proposed directive on approximation of laws relating to distortions of competition, relating to the terms and conditions of workers with atypical employment contracts. Commission proposal of 13 June 1990, COM (90) 228.

● Proposed directive on improving the health and safety at work of temporary workers. Commission proposal of 13 June 1990 COM (90) 228. (These latter three proposed directives replace the draft directive on voluntary part-time work, amended in 1983, and the draft directive on temporary work, amended in 1984.)

● Proposed directive on the protection of pregnancy at work, December 1990. Draft directive agreed on 6 November 1991.

RESOLUTIONS

These are non-binding statements of policy and include:

● Equality Action Programme 1982–5 – Community Action programme of equal opportunities for women approved and accompanied by Council Resolution on 27 May 1982.

● Equality Action Programme 1986–90 – Second Community action programme on the promotion of equal opportunities for women submitted to Council in December 1985, followed by Council Resolution of 5 July 1986, *Bulletin of the ECs*, Supplement 3/86.

● Unemployment among women – to combat unemployment among women, Council Resolution of 7 June 1984.

● Local Employment Initiatives – Council Resolution on the contribution of local employment initiatives to combating unemployment, 7 June 1984. Followed up by Commission Communication to Council, noted by the Council 7 June 1984.

● Dignity at Work – Council Resolution on the protection of the dignity of women and men at work – adopted by the Council on 29 May 1990. *Official Journal* C157 27.6.90, p. 3.

● Equality Action Programme 1991–5 – Third Community action programme on the promotion of equal opportunities for women submitted to the Council January 1991, COM (90) 499.

RECOMMENDATIONS

These are also non-binding and include:

● Reduction and reorganisation of working time – proposed Council Recommendation submitted to Council of Ministers on 16 September 1983, but rejected on 7 June 1984 because of UK veto.

● Positive Discrimination – Council Recommendation on the promotion of positive action for women, 13 December 1984.

● Vocational training for women, based on Commission's Communication of April 1987, adopted by the Council on 24 November 1987.

● Proposed recommendation on childcare, 1991.

● Proposed recommendation on pregnancy and maternity provisions, 1991.

Appendix 4: The Effect of Infringement Proceedings Against Member States to Implement the 1975 Equal Pay Directive

In Belgium the way that pay was defined through head-of-household allowances in the 1975 Collective Labour Agreement was seen to fall short of EC provisions. Infringements were withdrawn following the removal of the head-of-household allowances.

In Greece all workers have the right to equal pay for work of equal value (Article 22 of the Greek Constitution). In order to harmonise Greek law with the Directive the Government passed legislation on 10 February 1975.

In West Germany the 1980 law introducing the principle of equal pay for work of equal value did not, in the Commission's view, bring Germany in line with the Directive. Infringement proceedings were eventually heard by the European Court of Justice in May 1985, although the Court only accepted one of the Commission's five complaints.

In France infringement proceedings centred on head-of-household housing allowances but were dropped when new legislation was introduced in 1979 to remove this provision. New legislation was introduced in 1983 to strengthen women's rights at work.

In Luxembourg, the existence of a head-of-household allowance for state employees led to the European Court of Justice ruling against Luxembourg in July 1982. A law amending the Grand-Ducal Regulation of 1974 was introduced in 1982 to meet the objectives of the Directive.

In The Netherlands infringement proceedings were dropped with the introduction of a new law in 1980. This extended the right to equal pay in the public services (previously excluded from the 1975 law providing equal pay for work of equal value).

In Ireland the 1974 Anti Discrimination (Pay) Act was in line with the Directive. The 1975 Anti-Discrimination (Pay Amendment) Act postponed the application of the principle in certain female dominated industries. The

Commission refused to give Ireland the permission to go ahead with the 1975 Act. The Employment Equality Act of 1977 extended the principle of equal pay to all sectors.

In Denmark the 1976 law entitled men and women to the same rates of pay for like work, if not already covered by a collective agreement. However, this concept of equal work was seen to be too restrictive. Infringement proceedings were lodged by the Commission in July 1983.

In Italy the law of 9 December 1977 was seen to incorporate fully the concept of equal pay for work of equal value. It provided that 'female employees are entitled to receive the same pay as male employees for identical work or work of equal value'.

In the UK the Equal Pay Act 1970 was seen to fall short of the Directive. Infringement proceedings were brought against the Government in 1981, and in 1984 the Equal Pay Act was amended to incorporate the principle of equal pay for work of equal value.

Appendix 5: Cases in the English Courts that have been Affected by the Scope of EC Law

ARTICLE 119 AND THE 1975 EQUAL PAY DIRECTIVE

The effect of EEC law

Defrenne v. *Sabena* [1979] ECR, 455; *E. Coomes (Holdings) Ltd* v. *Shields* [1981] IRLR 263, CA; *Jenkins* v. *Kingsgate (Clothing Productions) Ltd* [1981] IRLR 228, ECJ; *Worringham* v. *Lloyds Bank* Ltd [1981] IRLR 178, ECJ; *Pickstone* v. *Freemans plc* [1988] IRLR 357, HL.

Meaning of 'pay'

Garland v. *British Rail Engineering Ltd* [1982] IRLR 111, ECJ; *Hammersmith & Queen Charlottes Special Health Authority* v. *Cato* [1987] IRLR 483, EAT.

Pension schemes

Bilka-Kaufhas GmgH v. *Weber von Hartz* [1986] IRLR 317, ECJ; *Newstead* v. *Department of Transport* [1988] IRLR 66, ECJ; *Worringham* v *Lloyds Bank Ltd* [1981] IRLR 178, ECJ; *Barber* v. *Guardian Royal Exchange Assurance Group*, ECJ, 14.5.90.

Redundancy payment

Hammersmith & Queen Charlottes Special Health Authority v. *Cato* [1987] IRLR 483, EAT.

Travel facilities

Garland v. *British Rail Engineering Ltd* [1982] IRLR 111, ECJ.

Choice of comparator

Macarthys Ltd v. *Smith* [1980] IRLR 210, ECJ.

Equal value

Bromley v. *H. & J. Quick Ltd* [1988] IRLR 249, CA; *Commission of the European Communities* v. *United Kingdom of Great Britain and Northern Ireland* [1982] IRLR 333, ECJ; *Clwyd County Council* v. *Leverton* [1985] IRLR 197, EAT; *Hayward* v. *Cammell Laird Shipbuilders Ltd* [1988] IRLR 257, HL; *Dennehy* v. *Sealink UK Ltd* [1987] 120, EAT; *Murphy* v. *Bord Telecome Eireann* [1988] IRLR 267, ECJ; *Pickstone* v. *Freemans plc* [1988] IRLR 357, HL; *Rummler* v. *Dato-Druck GmgH* [1987] 32, ECJ.

Burden of proof

Handels-og Kontorfunktionaerers Forbund i Danmark v. *Dask Arbejdsgiverforening (acting for Danfoss)*, ECJ, 17.9.89.

1976 EQUAL TREATMENT DIRECTIVE

Marshall v. *Southampton and South-West Hampshire Area Health Authority (Teaching)* 26.2.86; *Joan Roberts* v. *Tate & Lyle Industries Ltd* 26.2.86 (Case 151/84); *M. Johnston* v. *Chief Constable of Royal Ulster Constabulary*, 15.5.86 (Case 222/84).

1978 EQUALITY IN SOCIAL SECURITY DIRECTIVE

Jacqueline Drake v. *The Adjudication Officer* 24.6.86 (Case 150/85).

Appendix 6: Community Charter of Fundamental Social Rights of Workers

TITLE I – FUNDAMENTAL SOCIAL RIGHTS OF WORKERS

Freedom of movement

1. Every worker of the European Community shall have the right to freedom of movement throughout the territory of the Community, subject to restrictions justified on grounds of public order, public safety or public health.

2. The right to freedom of movement shall enable any worker to engage in any occupation or profession in the Community in accordance with the principles of equal treatment as regards access to employment, working conditions and social protection in the host country.

3. The right to freedom of movement shall also imply:

(i) harmonization of conditions of residence in all Member States, particularly those concerning family reunification;
(ii) elimination of obstacles arising from the non-recognition of diplomas or equivalent occupational qualifications;
(iii) improvement of the living and working conditions of frontier workers.

Employment and remuneration

4. Every individual shall be free to choose and engage in an occupation according to the regulations governing each occupation.

5. All employment shall be fairly remunerated. To this end, in accordance with arrangements applying in each country:

(i) workers shall be assured of an equitable wage, i.e. a wage sufficient to enable them to have a decent standard of living;
(ii) workers subject to terms and conditions of employment other than an open-ended full-time contract shall benefit from an equitable reference wage;
(iii) wages may be withheld, seized or transferred only in accordance with national law; such provisions should entail measures enabling the worker concerned to continue to enjoy the necessary means of subsistence for him or herself and his or her family.

190

6. Every individual must be able to have access to public placement services free of charge.

Improvement of living and working conditions

7. The completion of the internal market must lead to an improvement in the living and working conditions of workers in the European Community. This process must result from an approximation of these conditions while the improvement is being maintained, as regards in particular the duration and organization of working time and forms of employment other than open-ended contracts, such as fixed-term contacts, part-time working, temporary work and seasonal work.

The improvement must cover, where necessary, the development of certain aspects of employment regulations such as procedures for collective redundancies and those regarding bankruptcies.

8. Every worker of the European Community shall have a right to a weekly rest period and to annual paid leave, the duration of which must be progressively harmonized in accordance with national practices.

9. The conditions of employment of every worker in the European Community shall be stipulated in laws, a collective agreement or a contract of employment, according to arrangements applying in each country.

Social protection

According to the arrangements applying in each country:

10. Every worker of the European Community shall have a right to adequate social protection and shall, whatever his status and whatever the size of the undertaking in which he is employed, enjoy an adequate level of social security benefits.

Persons who have been unable either to enter or re-enter the labour market and have no means of subsistence must be able to receive sufficient resources and social assistance in keeping with their particular situation.

Freedom of association and collective bargaining

11. Employers and workers of the European Community shall have the right of association in order to constitute professional organizations or trade unions of their choice for the defence of their economic and social interests.

Every employer and every worker shall have the freedom to join or not to join such organizations without any personal or occupational damage being thereby suffered by him.

12. Employers or employers' organizations, on the one hand, and workers' organizations, on the other, shall have the right to negotiate and conclude collective agreements under the conditions laid down by national legislation and practice.

The dialogue between the two sides of industry at European level which must be developed, may, if the parties deem it desirable, result in contractual relations in particular at inter-occupational and sectoral level.

13. The right to resort to collective action in the event of a conflict of interests shall include the right to strike, subject to the obligations arising under national regulations and collective agreements.

In order to facilitate the settlement of industrial disputes the establishment and utilization at the appropriate levels of conciliation, mediation and arbitration procedures should be encouraged in accordance with national practice.

14. The internal legal order of the Member States shall determine under which conditions and to what extent the rights provided for in Articles 11 to 13 apply to the armed forces, the police and the civil service.

Vocational training

15. Every worker of the European Community must be able to have access to vocational training and to benefit therefrom throughout his working life. In the conditions governing access to such training there may be no discrimination on grounds of nationality.

The competent public authorities, undertakings or the two sides of industry, each within their own sphere of competence, should set up continuing and permanent training systems enabling every person to undergo retraining, more especially through leave for training purposes, to improve his skills or to acquire new skills, particularly in the light of technical developments.

Equal treatment for men and women

16. Equal treatment for men and women must be assured. Equal opportunities for men and women must be developed.

To this end, action should be intensified to ensure the implementation of the principle of equality between men and women as regards in particular access to employment, remuneration, working conditions, social protection, education, vocational training and career development.

Measures should also be developed enabling men and women to reconcile their occupational and family obligations.

Information, consultation and participation of workers

17. Information, consultation and participation of workers must be developed along appropriate lines, taking account of the practices in force in the various Member States.

These shall apply especially in companies or groups of companies having establishments or companies in two or more Member States of the European Community.

18. Such information, consultation and participation must be implemented in due time, particularly in the following cases:

(i) when technological changes which, from the point of view of working conditions and work organization, have major implications for the workforce, are introduced into undertakings;
(ii) in connection with restructuring operations in undertakings or in cases of mergers having an impact on the employment of workers;
(iii) in cases of collective redundancy procedures;
(iv) when transfrontier workers in particular are affected by employment policies pursued by the undertaking where they are employed.

Health protection and safety at the workplace

19. Every worker must enjoy satisfactory health and safety conditions in his working environment. Appropriate measures must be taken in order to achieve further harmonization of conditions in this area while maintaining the improvements made.

These measures shall take account, in particular, of the need for the training, information, consultation and balanced participation of workers as regards the risks incurred and the steps taken to eliminate or reduce them.

The provisions regarding implementation of the internal market shall help to ensure such protection.

Protection of children and adolescents

20. Without prejudice to such rules as may be favourable to young people, in particular those ensuring their preparation for work through vocational training, and subject to derogations limited to certain light work, the minimum employment age must not be lower than the minimum school leaving age and, in any case, not lower than 15 years.

21. Young people who are in gainful employment must receive equitable remuneration in accordance with national practice.

22. Appropriate measures must be taken to adjust labour regulations applicable to young workers so that their specific development and vocational training and access to employment needs are met.

The duration of work must, in particular, be limited – without it being possible to circumvent this limitation through recourse to overtime – and night work prohibited in the case of workers of under 18 years of age, save in the case of certain jobs laid down in national legislation or regulations.

23. Following the end of compulsory education, young people must be entitled to receive initial vocational training of a sufficient duration to enable them to adapt to the requirements of their future working life; for young workers, such training should take place during working hours.

Elderly persons

According to the arrangements applying in each country:

24. Every worker of the European Community must, at the time of retirement be able to enjoy resources affording him or her a decent standard of living.

25. Every person who has reached retirement age but who is not entitled to a pension or who does not have other means of subsistence must be entitled to sufficient resources and to medical and social assistance specifically suited to his needs.

Disabled persons

26. All disabled persons, whatever the origin and nature of their disablement, must be entitled to additional concrete measures aimed at improving their social and professional integration.

These measures must concern, in particular, according to the capacities of the beneficiaries, vocational training, ergonomics, accessibility, mobility, means of transport and housing.

TITLE II – IMPLEMENTATION OF THE CHARTER

27. It is more particularly the responsibility of the Member States in accordance with national practices, notably through legislative measures or collective agreements, to guarantee the fundamental social rights in this Charter and to implement the social measures indispensable to the smooth operation of the internal market as part of a strategy of economic and social cohesion.

28. The European Council invites the Commission to submit as soon as possible initiatives which fall within its powers, as provided for in the Treaties, with a view to the adoption of legal instruments for the effective implementation, as and when the internal market is completed, of those rights which come within the Community's area of competence.

29. The Commission shall establish each year, during the last three months, a report on the application of the Charter by the Member States and by the European Community.

30. The report of the Commission shall be forwarded to the European Council, the European Parliament and the Economic and Social Committee.

Bibliography

Agence Europe (1991) *Documents No. 1722/1723*, 5 July.

Allen, S. and C. Wolkowitz (1987) *Homeworking: Myths and Realities* (London: Macmillan).

Atkins, S. (1983) 'Equal Pay for Work of Equal Value', *Public Law*, Spring.

Banking, Insurance and Finance Union, *Equal Pay for Work of Equal Value* (London: BIFU, undated).

Belmont European Policy Centre (1991) *From Luxembourg to Maastricht: 100 Critical Days for Europe* (Brussels).

Bisset, L. and U. Huws (1984) *Sweated Labour: Homeworking in Britain Today*, Low Pay Unit Pamphlet, no. 33.

Boston, S. (1987) *Women Workers and Trade Unions*, 2nd edn (London: Lawrence & Wishart).

British Labour Group Women (1984) *Campaigning for Women's Rights in the European Elections* (Brussels: 14 January).

Buron, M. (1989) *Report on the Community Charter of Fundamental Social Rights* A3-69/89 (European Parliament).

Cameron, I. (1990) 'Banking and Financial Services 1992' in *Women and the Completion of the Internal Market*, Report and Conclusions of Dublin Seminar (Department of Labour, Dublin: Commission of the EC).

Cecchini Report, (1988) *The European Challenge 1992: The Benefits of a Single Market* (Aldershot: Wildwood House).

Centre for Research on European Women, *CREW Reports*, vol. 3, no. 10; vol. 5, no. 11; vol. 6, no. 6; vol. 6, no. 10, vol. 7, no. 7 (Brussels: CREW).

Clarke, L. (1983) 'Proposed Amendments to Equal Pay Act 1970', *New Law Journal*, 21 October.

Clarke, L. (1984) 'Equal Pay for Work of Equal Value', *New Law Journal*, 24 February 1984.

Cochrane, J. and E. Donnelly (1984) *Report on a Comparative Analysis of the Provisions for Legal Redress in Member States of the European Economic Community in Respect of Art. 119 and the Equal Pay, Equal Treatment and Social Security Directives*, prepared by the EOC for the EC Advisory Committee on Equal Opportunities for Men and Women (Brussels: Commission of the EC).

Collins, D. (1975) *The European Communities: The Social Policy of the European Economic Community 1958–1972* (London: Martin Robertson).

Collins, D. (1983) 'The Impact of Social Policy in the UK', in A. El-Agraa (ed.), *Britain within the European Community* (London: Macmillan).

Commission of the European Communities (1962) *EEC Bulletin*, no. 1.

Commission of the European Communities (1966) Report of 31 November, *EEC Bulletin*, no. 2.

Commission of the European Communities (1970a) *Rapport de la Commission au Conseil sur l'état d'application au 31 décembre 1968 au principe d'égalite entre rémunérations masculines et feminines*, SEC (70) 2338 final (Brussels).

195

Commission of the European Communities (1970b) *Bulletin of the European Communities*, no. 1.

Commission of the European Communities (1974a) *Report of the Commission to the Council on the application of the principle of equal pay for men and women* (Brussels).

Commission of the European Communities (1974b) *Women's Employment in the UK, Ireland and Denmark* (Brussels).

Commission of the European Communities (1974c) *Explanatory Memorandum for proposal for Council Directive on equal pay* COM (74) 1010 (Brussels: Commission of the EC, 3 July).

Commission of the European Communities (1974d) *Bulletin of the European Communities*, no. 2.

Commission of the European Communities (1975) *European Men and Women: A Comparison of their Attitudes to Some of the Problems Facing Society* (Brussels).

Commission of the European Communities (1978) *Education Action Programme at Community level: equal opportunities in education and training for girls* COM (78) 499 final, 3 October.

Commission of the European Communities (1979) *Report of the Commission to the Council on the application as at 12 February 1978 on the principle of equal pay for men and women.* COM (78) 711 final (Brussels, 16 January).

Commission of the European Communities (1980) *Women in the European Community: Community Action and Comparative National Situations* (Brussels).

Commission of the European Communities (1981) *Indirect Discrimination by Use of Job Classification Systems*, Working Paper (Brussels, March).

Commission of the European Communities (1984) 'Women at Work in the European Community', *Women of Europe*, supplement 15 (Brussels).

Commission of the European Communities (1985) *Report on the implementation of the new Action Programme* COM (85) 641 final (Brussels).

Commission of the European Communities (1986) 'Equal Opportunities: 2nd Action Programme 1986–90', *Women of Europe*, supplement 23, Brussels.

Commission of the European Communities (1987a) 'The Single Act: A New Frontier for Europe', reprinted in *Bulletin of the European Communities*, supplement 1/87.

Commission of the European Communities (1987b) 'Community Law and Women', *Women of Europe*, supplement 25, 152/87-EN (Brussels).

Commission of the European Communities (1988) *The 'cost of non-Europe' in financial services*, CB-PP-88-J14-EN-C.

Commission of the European Communities (1989a) *Employment in Europe* (Luxembourg).

Commission of the European Communities (1989b) *The 'cost of non-Europe' in the textiles/clothing industry* CB-PP-88-014-EN.

Commission of the European Communities (1989c) *Lone-Parent Families in the European Community*, Final Report, prepared by the Family Policy Studies Centre.

Commission of the European Communities (1989d) *Childcare and equality of Opportunity*, Report of European Childcare Network (Brussels).

Commission of the European Communities (1989e) *Communication from the Commission concerning its Action Programme relating to the implementation of the Community Charter of Basic Social Rights for Workers* COM (89) 568 final, November.

Commission of the European Communities (1989f) *Women in Atypical Employment*, Final Report by D. Meulders and R. Plasman, V/1426/89/ (Brussels).

Commission of the European Communities (1990a) *Employment in Europe* (Luxembourg).

Commission of the European Communities (1990b) *The Impact of the Completion of the Internal Market on Women in the European Community*, working document prepared by Pauline Conroy-Jackson for the Equal Opportunities Unit.

Commission of the European Communities (1990c) *Social Europe*, no. 1.

Commission of the European Communities (1990d) SEC (90) 1570 final, August.

Commission of the European Communities (1990e) Background Report, *Equal Opportunities for Men and Women: Third Action Programme*, London office, ISEC/B33/90.

Conroy-Jackson P. (1990) 'The Labour Market Effects of 1992 on Women' in *Women and the Completion of the Internal Market*, Report and Conclusions of Dublin Seminar (Department of Labour, Dublin/Commission of the EC).

Confederation of British Industry (1982) *CBI Comments on Department of Employment's Proposals for Amending Equal Pay Act* (London: CBI).

Confederation of British Industry (1983a) *CBI Response to Department of Employment's Consultative Draft Order* L.289 83/MEO-72, Social Affairs Directorate (London: CBI).

Confederation of British Industry (1983b) *CBI Response to Department of Employment's Draft Procedural Regulations on Equal Pay* L 778.83 (London: CBI).

Cook D., P. Gordon *Whose Europe?* (London: Refugee Forum).

Council of Ministers (1962) 'Council Resolution on the Implementation of Article 119, 1961', *EEC Bulletin*, no. 1.

Council of Ministers (1974a) 'Four Year Social Action Programme', *Official Journal* C 13, 12.2.74.

Council of Ministers (1974b) *Note on proposal for a Council Directive on the approximation of the laws of Member States relating to the application of the principle of equal pay for men and women contained in Article 119 of the EEC Treaty*, Report by the Working Party on Social Questions to the Permanent Representatives Committee, Doc R/2809/74 (SOC 235) (Brussels, 4 November).

Council of Ministers (1974c) *Note on proposal for a Council Directive on the approximation of the laws of Member States relating to the application of the principle of equal pay for men and women contained in Article 119 of the EEC Treaty*, Report by the Working Party on Social Questions to the Permanent Representatives Committee, R/2937/74 (SOC 246) (Brussels, 20 November).

Dale J. and P. Foster (1986) *Feminists and State Welfare* (London: Routledge & Kegan Paul).

Department of Employment (1982) *Specification for amending the Equal Pay Act, to provide for equal pay for men and women for work to which equal value is attributed* (London: Department of Employment, 12 August).

Department of Employment (1983a) *Supplementary Explanatory Memorandum on European Community Legislation* (London: Department of Employment, February).

Department of Employment (1983b) 'Consultation on Equal Pay Amendment' Press Notice, 16 February.

Department of Employment (1983c) 'Equal Pay Act – Amendment' Press Notice, 12 May.

Department of Employment (1983d) *Draft Statutory Instruments, The Equal Pay (Amendment Regulations) 1983: Draft Regulations laid before Parliament under paragraph 2 (2) of the European Communities Act, 1972, for approval by resolution of each House of Parliament* (London: Department of Employment, February).

Deshormes La Valle, F. (1979) 'The Women's Press and Organisations Department of the EEC Commission', *European Women about Europe* (Brussels; Ministry of Foreign Affairs, External Trade and Cooperation in Development).

Dickens, L., B. Townley and D. Winchester (1988) *Tackling Sex Discrimination Through Collective Agreements* (London: HMSO).

EEPTU (1984) 'Equal Pay for Work of Equal Value', *Women Workers Bulletin*, no. 3 (London: EEPTU, April).

Enloe, C. (1989) *Making Feminist Sense of International Politics* (London).

Equal Opportunities Commission (1982a) *Proposed Amendments to the Sex Discrimination Act, 1975 and the Equal Pay Act, 1970* (Manchester: EOC).

Equal Opportunities Commission (1982b) *Consultative Document: Equal Pay for Work of Equal Value* (Manchester: EOC).

Equal Opportunities Commission (1983a) *Leading Counsel's Opinion on the Proposed Amendments to the Equal Pay Act 1970* (Manchester: EOC, March).

Equal Opportunities Commission (1983b) *Response to the Draft Order to Amend the Equal Pay Act, 1970* (Manchester: EOC, 28 February).

Equal Opportunities Commission (1984a) *Job Evaluation Schemes Free from Sex Bias* (Manchester: EOC).

Equal Opportunities Commission (1984b) *Ninth Annual Report* (London: HMSO).

Equal Opportunities Commission (1985) *Tenth Annual Report* (London: HMSO).

Equal Opportunities Commission (1986) *Eleventh Annual Report* (London: HMSO).

Equal Opportunities Commission (1987) *Twelth Annual Report* (London: HMSO).

Equal Opportunities Commission (1988a) *Collective Bargaining: The Commonsense Way to End Sex Discrimination at work*, Press Release (Manchester: EOC, 2 August).

Equal Opportunities Commission (1988b) *Negotiating for Equality* (Manchester: EOC).

Equal Opportunities Commission (1989) *Equal Pay: Making it Work* (Manchester: EOC).

Equal Opportunities Review, January/February 1990, July/August 1990, September/October 1990.

Equal Pay and Opportunity Campaign (1983) *Comments on Draft Order to Amend the Equal Pay Act* (London: EPOC).

Esping-Andersen, G. (1990) *The Three Worlds of Welfare Capitalism* (Oxford: Polity Press).

European Community Treaties (1977) 3rd edn (London: Sweet & Maxwell).

European Network of Women (UK Section) (1989) *Comments on the Draft Proposals for an EEC Women's Lobby* (London: January).

European Trade Union Confederation (1988) *Creating the European Social Dimension in the Internal Market* (Brussels: ETUC).

European Trade Union Confederation (1990) Women's Committee *Women in Europe – The Social Aspects: Comments on the List of Demands* (Brussels: ETUC).

European Parliament (1976) 'Debates in the European Parliament, 1975–6 Session', Report of Proceedings of 10–14 May 1976, Strasbourg. *Official Journal* no. 203, May 1976.

European Parliament (1978a) 'Debates in the European Parliament, 1977–8 Session', Report of Proceedings from 13–17 February, 1978, Strasbourg. *Official Journal* no 226, February 1978.

European Parliament (1978b) 'Interim Report drawn up by the Committee on Social Affairs, Employment and Education on equal pay for men and women in the Member States of the Community', rapporteur Mrs G Dunwoody, *European Parliament Working Documents*, Document 6/78, PE 50.717/fin (Luxembourg, 22 March).

European Parliament (1979a) 'Report drawn up on behalf of the Committee on Social Affairs, Employment and Education on equal pay for men and women in the Member States of the Community', rapporteur Mrs G. Dunwoody, *European Parliament Working Documents*, Document 6/78, PE 56.361/fin (Luxembourg).

European Parliament (1979b) 'Debates in the European Parliament, 1979–80 Session', Report of Proceedings of 7–11 May 1979 (Luxembourg) *Official Journal* no. 243, May 1979.

European Parliament (1979c) 'Equal pay for men and women in the Member States of the Community', *European Parliament Working Documents*, Report PE 50.717/fin, rapporteur Mrs G. Dunwoody (Luxembourg, 2 May 1979).

European Parliament (1980) 'Interim Report drawn up on behalf of the Committee on Social Affairs and Employment on the position of women in the European Community', rapporteur Mrs S. Dekker, *European Parliament Working Documents*, Document 1/78/80, PE 63.679/fin (Luxembourg).

European Parliament (1981a) 'Debates in the European Parliament', Verbatim report of proceedings (Strasbourg, 10–12 January).

European Parliament (1981b) The Position of Women in the European Community: European Parliament Debates (collection of texts), Directorate General for Research and Documentation, European Parliament (Luxembourg).

European Parliament (1981c) 'Report drawn up on behalf of the Ad Hoc Committee on Women's Rights on the position of women in the European Community' rapporteur Mrs Hanja Maij-Weggen, *European Parliament Working Documents*, Document 1-829/80, PE 67.021/fin (Luxembourg, 29 January).

European Parliament (1982) 'Report drawn up on behalf of the Committee on Social Affairs and Employment on the proposal from the Commission for a directive on voluntary part-time work', *European Parliament Working Documents*, Document 1-540/82, PE 77.691/fin, 3 September.

European Parliament (1983a) 'Report tabled by the Committee of Inquiry into the Situation of Women on the situation of women in Europe', *European Parliament Working Documents* Document 1-1229/83.

European Parliament (1983b) Report by Gaiotti de Biase, 'Implementation of the Directive on Equal Pay', Report of the Committee of Inquiry into the Situation of Women in Europe, *European Parliament Working Documents*, Document 1-1229/83/C, PE 86.199/fin/C.

European Parliament (1984a) Debates in the European Parliament no. 1-308, 17.1.84 (Luxembourg).

European Parliament (1984b) 'Report drawn up on behalf of the Committee on Social Affairs and Employment on the proposal from the Commission to the Council for a directive on parental leave and leave for family reasons', *European Parliament Working Documents*, Document 1-1528/83, PE.271/fin (Luxembourg, 15 March).

European Parliament (1985) Committee of Inquiry into the Rise of Fascism and Racism in Europe, *Report of the Findings of the Inquiry*.

European Parliament (1988) Committee on Women's Rights *Working document on the effects of the completion of the internal market in 1992 on women in Europe*, rapporteur M. Van Hemeldonck, PE 125.071.

European Parliament (1990a) Report of the Committee of Social Affairs, Employment and the Working Environment, *On the communication from the Commission on its Action Programme relating to the implementation of the Community Charter of fundamental social rights for workers – priorities for the period 1991–2*, PE 140.000/fin, 4 July.

European Parliament (1990b) *Report on behalf of the Committee of Inquiry into Racism and Xenophobia on the findings of the Committee*, rapporteur Glyn Ford, October.

European Parliament (1990c) *Motion for a Resolution on a Community definition of equality of opportunity and discrimination*, PE 139.857, 8.3.90.

Eurostat (1985) *Labour Force Survey* (Luxembourg: Statistical Office of the EC).

Fawcett Society (1983) *Report on a Conference on Equal Pay for Work of Equal Value*, 12 February.

Feminist Review (ed.) (1986) *Waged Work: A Reader* (London: Virago).

Ghobadian, A. and M. White (1987) 'Job Evaluation and Equal Pay', *Department of Employment Research Paper no 58* (London: HMSO).

Glendinning, C. and J. Millar (eds) (1987) *Women and Poverty in Britain* (Brighton: Harvester).

Goldsmith, J. (1990) *The Effects on Women of the European Internal Market in 1992, with Particular Reference to the Problems for Black and Ethnic Minority Women in the UK*, Report prepared for Anita Pollack, MEP.

Gordon, P. (1989) *Fortress Europe? The Meaning of 1992* (London: Runneymead Trust).

Graham, C. and N. Lewis (1985) *The Role of ACAS Conciliation in Equal Pay and Sex Discrimination Cases* (Manchester: EOC).

Holloway, D. J. (1981) *Social Policy Harmonisation in the European Community* (Farnborough: Gower).

Hoskyns, C. (1986) 'Women's Equality and the European Community' in Feminist Review (ed) *Waged Work: A Reader* (London: Virago).

Hoskyns, C. (1988) ' "Give Us Equal Pay and We'll Open Our Own Doors": A Study of the Impact in the Federal Republic of Germany and the Republic of Ireland of the European Community's Policy on Women's Rights', in M. Buckley and M. Anderson (eds) *Women, Equality and Europe* (Basingstoke: Macmillan).

House of Commons, *Hansard*, Second Reading of the Equal Pay Bill, vol. 823, 9 February 1970.

House of Lords, *Hansard*, Issue no 1233 5–8 December 1983.

House of Commons, *Hansard*, Issue no 1292, 9 December 1983.

House of Lords (1982) Select Committee on the European Communities, *Voluntary Part-time Work*, Session 1981–2, 19th Report (London: HMSO).

House of Lords (1989) Select Committee on the European Communities, *Equal Treatment for Men and Women in Pensions and other Benefits*, Session 1988–9, 10th Report (London: HMSO).

Huws, U. (1989) 'Danger: Women at Work', *New Statesman & Society*, 17 March, p. 12.

Income Data Services (1982) 'Part-Timers: Problems and Practice', *IDS Study*, no. 267, June.

International Labour Organisation (1979) *List of Major ILO Instruments and Documents Concerning Women Workers* (Geneva: ILO).

IRLIB (1983) 'Equal Value Claims' *IRLIB*, no. 225, 25 January.

Labour Research Department (1986) *Women's Pay: Claiming Equal Value* (London: LRD).

Labour Research Department (1990) *Europe's Unions Women, March* (London: LRD).

Laffan, B. (1983) 'Policy Implementation in the European Community: The Social Fund as a Case Study', *Journal of Common Market Studies*, vol. XXI, no. 4, June.

Land, H. (1980) 'The Family Wage', *Feminist Review*, no. 6.

Land, H. (1981) *Parity Begins at Home: Women's and Men's Work in the Home and Its Effects on Their Paid Employment* (Manchester: EOC, September).

Langan, M. and I. Ostner, (1990) *Gender and Welfare: Towards a Comparative Framework*, Paper presented to the 1990 Social Policy Association Annual Conference, Bath, p. 6.

Laufer, J. (1982) *Equal Opportunities in Banking in the Countries of the EEC* (Brussels: Commission of the European Communities).

Leibfried, S. (1990) *Income Transfers and Poverty Policy in EC Perspective: On Europe's Slipping into Anglo-American Welfare Models*, Paper Presented to

EC Seminar, 'Poverty, Marginalisation and Social Exclusion in the Europe of the 90s', Alghero, April 1990.

Lester, A. (1983) 'Unequal Pay – Unequal Justice', *New Law Journal*, 28 October.

Lester, A. and D. Wainwright (1984) *Equal Pay for Work of Equal Value: Law and Practice* (London: TMS Management Consultants).

Lestor, J. (1983) *British negotiations for voluntary part-time work*, Background note for PQ 0683 (London: House of Commons).

Lovenduski, J. (1986) *Women and European Politics* (Brighton: Wheatsheaf).

Lovenduski, J. (1988) 'The Women's Movement and Public Policy in Western Europe: Theory, Strategy, Practice and Politics', in M. Buckley and M. Anderson (eds), *Women, Equality and Europe* (London: Macmillan).

McNally, J. (1982) 'Job Evaluation, Equal Pay and the Trade Unions', *Equal Opportunities International* vol. 1, no. 4.

McCrudden, C. (1984) 'Equal Pay for Work of Equal Value', *The Industrial Law Journal*, vol. 13, no. 1, March.

Martin, J. and C. Roberts (1984) *Women and Employment: A Lifetime Perspective*, Report of the 1980 DE/OPCS Women and Employment Survey (London: HMSO).

Mayo, M. (ed) (1977) *Women in the Community* (London: Routledge & Kegan Paul).

Meeham, E. (1985) *Women's Rights at Work: Campaigns and Policy in Britain and the United States* (London: Macmillan).

Megahy, T. 'Retreat on the Social Charter', Socialist Group of the European Parliament, undated.

Morris, J. (1984) *No More Peanuts: An Evaluation of Women's Work*, (London: NCCL).

National Association of Local Government Officers (1983) *Equal Pay: NALGO's Response to the Government Proposals on European Court Ruling*, 95/RES/83 (London: NALGO, 27 April).

National Council for Civil Liberties (Rights of Women Unit) (1983) *Comments on DE proposals to introduce equal pay for work of equal value into the EqPA, 1970* (London: NCCL).

National Union of Public Employees, *Equal Value, Equal Pay: what it means for women in NUPE* (London: NUPE, undated).

Neilson, R. (1981) *Equality Legislation in a Comparative Perspective: Towards State Feminism* (Copenhagen: Women's Research Centre in Social Science, February).

Neuberger, H. (1989) *The Economics of 1992* (Socialist Group of the European Parliament).

Ohlin Report (1956) 'Social Aspects of European Economic Co-operation: Summary of the Group's Report', *International Labour Review*, no. 74.

PABB (1988) 'Equal value negotiations move slowly forward', *PABB*, no. 207, 5 May.

Pascall, G. (1986) *Social Policy: A Feminist Analysis* (London and New York: Tavistock).

Phillips, A. and P. Moss (1988) *Who Cares for Europe's Children* Report of the European Childcare Network (Brussels: Commission of the European Communities).

Phillips, A. and B. Taylor (1980) 'Sex and Skill: Notes Towards a Feminist Economics', *Feminist Review*, no. 6.

Pillinger, J. (1989) 'Women and 1992: Everything To Go For', *International Labour Reports* no. 34/35.

Povall, M. (1980) *Job Segregation: A Major Obstacle to Equality* (Brussels: Commission of the EC, April).

Purcell, K., S. Wood, A. Waton and S. Allen (1986) *The Changing Experience of Employment: Restructuring and Recession* (London: Macmillan).

Randall, V. (1987) *Women and Politics*, 2nd edn (London: Macmillan).

Rights of Women Europe Group (1980) *The EEC and Women – A Case Study of British and European Legislation on Equal Pay*, Paper presented to the 1980 PSA Women's Group Day Conference, 27 September.

Rights of Women Europe Group (1983) *Women's Rights and the EEC: A Guide for Women in the UK* (London: ROW).

Robbins Report (1952) *The Internal Financial Situation of Member and Associated Countries* (Paris: OEEC).

Rubenstein, M. (1983) 'Discriminatory Job Evaluation Schemes and the Equal Pay (Amendment) Regulations', *New Law Journal*, 18 November.

Rubenstein, M. (1984) *Equal Pay for Work of Equal Value: The New Regulations and their Implications* (London: Macmillan).

Rubenstein, M. (1988) 'Discrimination: A Guide to the Relevant Case Law on Race and Sex Discrimination and Equal Pay', *Industrial Relations Law Reports: Equal Opportunities Review*, 1st edn.

Rubenstein, M. (1989) *Dignity at Work* (Brussels: Commission of the EC).

Rubery, J. (ed) (1988) *Women and Recession* (London: Routledge & Kegan Paul).

Runneymead Trust (1987) *Combating Racism in Europe: A Summary of Alternative Approaches to the Problem of Protection Against Racism and Xenophobia in Member States of the European Community* (London: Runneymead Trust).

Schofield, P. G. (1982) 'Equal Pay for Work of Equal Value: Commission of the *European Communities v UK*', *Industrial Law Journal*, vol. 11, 4 December.

Segal, L. (ed) (1983) *What is to be done about the family?* (London: Penguin).

Sex Equality Bill (1983) House of Commons, *Hansard*, Issue no. 987, 20 July (presented by Jo Richardson).

Shanks, M. (1978) 'European Social Policy: The Next Stage', in B. Burrows, G. Denton and G. Edwards (eds), *Federal Solutions to European Issues* (London: Macmillan).

Shimmin, S. (1984) *Job Evaluation and Equal Pay for Work of Equal Value*, Paper given at the Third Research Conference of the European Committee on Work and Pay.

Socialist Group of the European Parliament (1991) *1992 Implications for Women in South Yorkshire*, Report by Norman West, MEP, Barnsley.

Spark Report (1956) *Comité Intergovernmental Crée par la Conference de Messina: Rapport des Chefs de Délégation aux Ministres des Affairs Etrangers* (Brussels).

Spencer, M. (1990) *1992 And All that: Civil Liberties in the Balance* (London: Civil Liberties Trust).

Squarcialupi, V. (1983) *Report on Sexual Discrimination at the Workplace* 1-1358/83 (European Parliament).

Sullerot, E. (1975) 'Equality of Remuneration in the EEC', *International Labour Review*, vol. 112, August/September.

Sullerot, E. (1979) *The Employment of Women and the Problems it Raises in the Member States of the European Community*, abridged and translated edition (Brussels: Commission of the EC).

Szyszcazak, E. (1984) 'Pay Inequalities and Equal Value Claims', *Modern Law Review* no. 48.

Szyszcazak, E. (1987) 'The Future of Women's Rights: The Role of European Community Law', *Yearbook of Social Policy 1986–7* (London: Longman).

Tatchell, P. (1990) *Out in Europe: A Guide to Lesbian and Gay Rights in 30 European Countries* (Channel Four, London).

Taylor, P. (1983) *The Limits of European Integration* (London: Croom Helm).

TUC (1980) *Proposed Amendments to the Equal Pay Act* (London: TUC, 2 December).

TUC (1981) *Women Workers: 1981, Report for 1980–1 of the TUC Women's Advisory Committee* (London: TUC).

TUC (1982) *52nd TUC Women's Conference, Report for 1981–2 of the TUC's Women's Advisory Committee* (London: TUC).

TUC (1983) *TUC's Response to the Government's Proposed Draft Order* (London: TUC).

TUC (1984) *Report of the 53rd TUC's Women's Conference* (London: TUC).

Ungerson, C. (1985) *Women and Social Policy: A Reader* (London: Macmillan).

Vallance, E. (1982) *Women and Politics* (London: Macmillan).

Von Prondzynski, F. (1987) *Implementation of the Equality Directives* (Luxembourg: Commission of the EC).

Walby, S. (1986) *Patriarchy at Work: Patriarchal and Capitalist Relations in Employment* (London: Polity Press).

Warner, H. (1984) 'EC Social Policy in Practice: Community Action on Behalf of Women and its Impact in the Member States' in *Journal of Common Market Studies*, vol. XXIII, no. 2, December.

Weir, A. and M. McIntosh (1982) 'Towards a Wages Strategy for Women', *Feminist Review*, vol. 10, Spring.

Williams, F. (1989) *Social Policy: A Critical Introduction* (Cambridge: Polity Press).

Willoughby, L. (1990) 'The Impact of 1992 on Women in Electronics and Computing: Training to Meet the Challenge', in *Women and the Completion of the Internal Market*, Report and Conclusions of Dublin Seminar (Department of Labour, Dublin: Commission of the EC).

Index

205

X